WISDOM'S CHUNK - 5 BOOKS IN 1

VOLUME 1

SINMISOLA OGÚNYINKA

THIS BOOK IS INSPIRED BY THE HOLY SPIRIT
WISDOM'S CHUNK
VOLUME 1

5 BOOKS IN 1
WISDOM FOR MEN
WISDOM FOR WOMEN
WISDOM FOR SINGLES
WISDOM FOR PASTORS
WISDOM FOR PASTORS' WIVES

WISDOM *for* MEN

Ec 9:16 ... "Wisdom is better than strength"

Dedicated to my father:

Dr. E. A. Ifaturoti (1920 – 2009)

A good man

CONTENTS

WISDOM FOR MEN

LIVING IN A TEMPTER'S WORLD

THE OHA SOUP TASTED exactly as Nonso loved it. He wondered what magic Uche had performed. Her Oha soup had usually been tolerated by him, just because he loved the soup. He understood quite alright. She had been raised by Yoruba people after losing her parents in a ghastly motor accident, and had never gotten the privilege of learning to cook the delicious Igbo soup. The family that took her in had been wonderful and had taken care of her for the twenty-three years before he met and married her. That was eight years ago. Her story had been so pathetic; he had loved her for being a survivor, a winner. Some other attributes of womanhood and kitchen etiquette were missing but who cared about that when there were so many good things to see in her.

"This is the sweetest Oha soup I have ever eaten in my life" he belched and Uche laughed, pleased.

"Let your mother hear that" she teased. "She'll skin you alive". The in-law problems between them had long since been labelled 'no go'.

"Who taught you to cook this?" he washed the delicious meal down with a glass of cold water and washed his hands in the soapy water provided.

"I didn't cook it. Uju did" she said.

"I wonder. She's good, though" Nonso said dryly.

"I don't know why you don't like that girl" Uche cleared the dishes in front of him. "Now you are enjoying her food"

"Pardon me, I'll do well without her food" he stood up and stretched. "I have men's meeting this evening. I'll see you when I come back"

"Ok" she said and finished up her chores. By the time she was through, he had left. So much for trying to give him a treat, she thought.

When Nonso came back from his meeting at about 7pm, Uche had gone out of the house and it was Uju that welcomed him. She was a fresh graduate Uche had taken a liking to, in the church choir where they both served. The first time she came home with Uche, Nonso had formed an impression about her; she was a tempter. A beautiful, curvy, fair-skinned lady, her well-endowed body was hardly concealed in the spaghetti-strap dress she wore. Nonso had a first quick glance and decided not to take a second look. It would have been too much on his male libido.

"Hi" she greeted with a soft voice.

"Where's Uche?" he asked, deliberately ignoring her greeting, or the tight jeans and transparent blouse she wore. Her anatomy was hard to overlook.

"She went for an emergency choir rehearsal" Uju replied. She had been cooking another pot of soup when Nonso came in. Now she leaned against the kitchen table and assessed her host. He was every woman's dream husband, handsome, rich, and spiritual. Uche could never under-stand what she had. Uju was sure of that because Uche talked to her all the time about even the intricate things in her marriage.

"She didn't tell me about it" Nonso said, wondering why. Why was Uju not in that meeting? Why would Uche leave Uju behind when she knew she was meant to be in the meeting too. He smelled a rat. Uju shrugged. Her posture was too suggestive. Her bosom was almost popping out of their transparent confines, the way she leaned over the kitchen table.

"Well" he turned to leave but she stopped him with a small cough.

"I wanted to see you" she said. He turned and noticed she was slightly bent over, causing havoc in his brain.

"Yes?" he trained his voice, his thought and his sight. It wouldn't work. She walked to stand in front of him and touched the front of his shirt. His hand shot up to hold her advance. "What do you want?"

"My mother is very sick and I need about fifty thousand naira to offset the bill. I can't think of anyone to ask... you are like a brother" she said, looking into his eyes with longing. With her dressed like this, he didn't feel anything like a brother, spiritual, fraternal or biological. He let her hand go and she slid it into the small opening at the base of his throat. Oh God, please! He moaned under his breath. He knew what to do; he should send her away at once. Or refer her to Uche about the money. But could he? His breath was caught in his throat, his tongue glued to the roof of his mouth. Uche could walk in any moment. Uju would kill him if he let her. He sighed and pulled her closer.

This world is the tempter's. The Bible says categorically that the devil is the god of this world and gone are the days when demons transform into angels of light tripping the children of God. Now the devil uses believers. His mission is to fall man, and he's working hard at it. My brother, I tell you, the demons afflicting you are right there with you. The bible tells us to flee every appearance of evil. Sometimes you need to pick your car keys or take a jog! Otherwise, she's there to kill, steal and destroy. She is in the choir, in the teaching ministry, in children's church, or even in the ministry team! She could be anywhere, married or not. When you see her brake light, throttle down. Women sometimes are careless, exposing their husbands to evil and temptation but it's not an excuse God will accept. Take it or leave it, you have to deal with the tempter yourself and win, because you live in his world but you've been made an overcomer.

The bottom line as Christian men is to remember John 16:33 and to strive prayerfully to be a partaker and to overcome every temptation by God's grace alone. May God help us.

Amen.

WISDOM FOR MEN

DEAD MAN WALKING

EVERYONE WHO KNEW THE Alejos knew the Alejos. Taiwo Alejo was a quiet, unassuming banker whose work often kept him out late at night. He worked very hard at what he did and believed in the Nigerian banking system. He also believed one day that he would start a bank of his own. He had it all planned out. He had a name for it, the number of people on his board and how it would be run. He even had some banking packages that he'd never seen any bank operate in. not that he was not loyal to his bank, he was. But after introducing some of these packages to the management and getting a 'nail' he'd kept his vision to himself. His wife, Martha had no identity anyone knew. When you ask her where's she's from, she would tell you she's a Nigerian. She spoke the major languages in the country fluently and associated freely. In her shop where she did her general merchandise, she was everything to everyone. An outgoing personality per excellence, she mixed without bias. She had a small sit-out eatery where she served pepper soup and all drinks excluding hots. Her boutique and supermarket was within the hairdressing salon. Martha moved within her own world and anyone seeing her may confuse her for someone else, depending on the mood you meet her. One minute, she's laughing, chatting and gossiping with her customers. The next minute she was slapping a member of her staff and the very next, entertaining her pastor with a bottle of malt and boasting of her ability to run a sit-out successfully without serving alcohol. The Alejo couple had three sons. Julian was the oldest, at fifteen years old. He was quiet like his father and sang in the church choir. Seemingly unassuming, Julian was popular amongst the ladies. He sent suggestive text messages and then denied it. Amongst the guys, he was a good guy. He gave money to his classmates as he had abundance of it, and with his mother's consent but not his father's knowledge. Jide was the second at age nine. Jide also had a handset his mother proudly got for him. It helped him to contact his daddy at all times and he did whatever he wished. Jide was the apple of his mother's eyes and that gave him the platform to misbehave. He lacked manners and was rude generally in church and at his mother's business place. Justin, the last at five years old was an invalid neither parent nor brothers liked to associate with. When he was three he had a falling accident and broke his spine, and since had remained bound to a wheel chair. He had a nurse who stayed with him 24/7 in the house. It was the low point of their family life; one, which Martha made sure, was well hidden in their picture-perfect life.

Looking back, after the ordeal, Taiwo had always seen it coming. His life was a farce. His wife was uncontrolled when she should have been. His children had little or no respect for anyone when they could have had. He had been too preoccupied with making it, and over-indulgent of his wife, inattentive to his children. He remembered clearly how it had all started when his wife needed to expand her business.

"You work in a bank, and yet, you live like a pauper" she said tartly.

"Bank money is not my money" he mumbled.

"That's what you said when I asked you for money to start the salon. I heard the same when I started the sit-out and still the same when I started the boutique. But have you died since then?"

"No but I've been running from one bank to the other, hopping from one city to another hoping record will not show when they can still see me…"

"And getting away with it"

She nagged him day and night. All she needed was one million naira. He argued that he had never taken more than a hundred thousand at a time. One million was going too far. But when he thought he would run away, he transferred the amount to her account, debiting the other account. She made a big noise about the new outlet, a full-blown restaurant. Five days after the restaurant started, Taiwo applied to go for his annual leave. It was approved. He had cold feet about that account even though he had taken the money from a seemingly docile account. He planned to have Martha pack her store and business gradual while he was on leave. They could start in a new environment in no time. But the bubble burst in his face before the week ran out. The owner of the docile account called in for his balance. If Taiwo had been on seat, he would have given the balance the man expected but the person sitting in for him gave away what he saw. The owner of the account was infuriated and called the manager to find out what was happening. All officers on leave were called back in. After much investigation, the lead became cold. There was no way to know who deducted the money from the account. They narrowed the suspects down and excluded Taiwo. He was too good a guy. Then something awful happened! Martha walked into the provision store owned by one of the customers of the bank and made some noise about people who thought they could intimidate her husband. The customer who was not privy to anything happening in the bank went snooping and gathered incriminating evidence pointing to Taiwo's three previous places of work. There would be an unsolvable theft from a seeming docile account, and by the time the owner showed up and made noise, Taiwo would be far away. The customer who had been hoping to receive some favour from the bank went to the manager with the information he had. The manager went to work, verifying. It was too true to be true. Taiwo Alejo had on three previous occasions in the three different banks he worked taken a sudden walk immediately after a computer theft. He took a leave and from there resigned.

Taiwo Alejo was arrested, charged and convicted of fraud for five different offences in five different banks. He was sentenced to twenty-five years in prison but after much haggling and appeals, he got five years. His wife left him and moved to another town before the case was over. She was able to escape with all the equipments she had gotten for her businesses. She took Julian and Jide with her. Justin was taken to live with his mother in the village.

———————❦———————

There are so many dead men walking on the streets. Many of them are in the church. They love their wives unto death, literally. But scriptures say we should love our wives as Christ loved us, giving Himself for us. To sanctify us, and to purify us and to present us blameless Eph. 5: 25-29. The scripture is so full of information and wisdom. By leaving that woman to do as she pleases, allowing her to manipulate you and dominate you, frustrate and intimidate you is by looking for your own destruction. Women love to be controlled and directed. Women need to be controlled and directed! When she starts asking for what is not convenient, put your feet down. She'll hate you for it but on the long run, you can both live like you are alive.

WISDOM FOR MEN

THAT'S MY GIRL

HARUNA HAD TWO GEARS only. One for business and the other for Halima. When he was switched on to business, he made a lot of money. When he switched to Halima, he made enemies. Halima, his first daughter was the apple of his eyes. After God was Halima and business in order of preference. He never could place where the love came from but largely; he attributed it to the similarities between Halima and his mother. Besides, she was his first daughter, his babbar-yata. From the very first moment she took her first breath, he had loved her. Until ten, his gear switched only for business. His beautiful wife, Aliya and son, Hassan were only part of necessities. Initially, he showed preference to Halima only because she was so adorable and he had been absent at her delivery, but as she grew, other things drew him to her. Halima was skin, bones and brains. The first few years of her education found her topping every class. Haruna found himself taking her everywhere and giving rules only when they suited Halima.

One rule was standard in their home. No one stayed out of the house after eight even on days they had to attend evening service, because the family had only one meal together daily, and that was dinner at eight. Halima was in the choir in church, and also in the dancing group even though her talents extended beyond this. She was a gifted artist also and had even done a portrait of her daddy, which he hung proudly in his office. She was also an orator, a poet and a prolific writer. She had settled for the course of her dreams, medicine even though her final exam result was so good in the art subjects her uncles struggled amongst themselves to get her to study accountancy and law. One of them even tried to encourage her to study an engineering course. Anyway, on this fateful day, the choir rehearsals extended and Halima walked into the house at a half past eight in the evening. The family was just rounding off dinner without her. Hassan looked at their father's face expecting heat. The face was stone cold expressionless. Aliya quietly excused herself as Halima rushed into her father's arms and hugged him.

"Daddy, I am so sorry. I couldn't get a taxi on time and…"

"Why didn't you take a car? My God, do you know the danger you expose yourself to taking taxis at night? How have you been attending these rehearsals before?" Haruna asked alarmed.

Halima shrugged and looked at Hassan guiltily. "Hassan used to drop me and pick me but he didn't show up today" she sulked.

"I was there quarter to eight you told me to come back later" Hassan fired. How could she try to blame this on him?

"But did you go back?" Haruna flared.

"Dad? I had a curfew to observe" he replied offended.

"Well, not today" Haruna said angrily. "So the curfew is more important to you than your sister's life"

"I…well, I apologise" he said and excused himself to his room, slamming the door. He remembered clearly an incident that happened a few months back when he had been caught in a riot on his way home. He hadn't been able to escape and had arrived well after eight. His father had seized his car for three months as his punishment. The eight o'clock curfew at home had been most important then. Not his life or the danger he had been exposed to, driving right into a heat of a riot in his bid to take a shorter cut to get back home for dinner.

He overheard Haruna cooing into Halima's ears and assuring her he would give her a car of her own on her eighteenth birthday which was just a few months away. He'd gotten his own car on his twenty-second birthday just the previous year, after he successfully graduated in law with a second class upper.

Men naturally feel 'something' special for their daughters, especially the first one and then if she ends up being the only girl. A friend of mine said he didn't want a daughter because if she doesn't come home on time, he would have a heart failure! What of your son? I asked and he said he can take care of himself. On the contrary, women would want to dote on the boy. It is not possible not to have preferences amongst the children and it will be unrealistic and foolish to admonish that we should love all our children equally. However, making the preference so obvious breeds enmity amongst the children. Often, you see these children taking advantage of the soft spot you have for them. Often, these children use that soft spot to manipulate you to get what they want. Why would one child ask another to 'please tell daddy for me' when they are both your children especially if they are both grown children. It is not healthy. One day, this same advantage they will use against one another and end up causing you unimaginable grief. In your old age, you want your children to surround you peaceably. You don't want to be settling sibling squabble and afraid your children will constantly be at par when you are gone. You don't want to imagine your children will litigate against one another over the way you shared your property to them after you are gone. More importantly, while you are still alive, you don't want your children to refuse to see one another face to face, refusing to visit with you when their siblings or a particular sibling is around. You can prevent all these heartaches by simple discipline. While they are still young and growing, make them understand that the soft spot you have for one is not going to be to the detriment of the other. As often as you say, 'that's my girl', be able to, also say 'that's my boy'!

WISDOM FOR MEN

DON'T YOU DARE TOUCH MY KIDS

KEYU STOOD QUIETLY AND waited for Komomoh's response. He was as uncomfortable about this whole issue as anyone in his condition could be. He knew he was past loving a woman and had made that as plain as he possibly could to Mom, as he fondly called her. All the same, he needed her consent. Her verbal agreement before he made it a law. They had gotten married just a few weeks earlier and his children had now come home for holidays.

"You know I will agree to whatever you say" she mumbled softly. "I have no choice" she shrugged.

"I don't want you to see it as anything. I… when we, if their mother was alive, we…" his throat constricted. He still could not talk about her without that forlorn feeling. Mom stared at him. "Discipline was, is an issue between us and I will appreciate it if, you can" he stammered. "I want to discipline my children, myself" he finished.

Mom shrugged and accepted the order in good faith.

Keyu had lost his wife of six years, leaving two children behind. It had been a painful experience for him. What would he do with two small children Jesam aged five and Janice, four. The two boys didn't even know what had happened to them. Keyu had been advised to remarry quickly, before the vacuum began to be felt. Keyu struggled with the idea. How could he just remarry after losing Mercy? He mourned her for a whole year and then accepted the suggestion of his family and friends. But after Mercy, he didn't have the slightest idea on how to approach a woman. His desire for women had died with his beloved wife. After desperate trial at meeting and marrying a woman in a time span of another two years, without much success, he was introduced to Komomoh. She was a beautiful, bubbly woman in her mid-thirties who had never been married. When she met Keyu, she liked him instantly but was not ready for a relationship. Keyu liked her too but constantly, subconsciously measured her up with Mercy. After much persuasion, he finally won Komomoh's heart. She knew she would be second best to him and that was her initial fear. He pleaded for her to understand his plight. It would not be easy to get over his first wife. She indulged him, but refused to allow him to keep memoirs around the house. The house was redecorated to her taste and wall photos neatly and carefully stacked away. Komomoh was excited about her new home and was ready to be mother to her two new sons. She even went as far as insisting that they be removed from boarding school, arguing that were still too young.

It was their first holiday with her at home. Jesam, now eight insisted on watching TV as soon as he woke up the following morning. Komomoh disagreed with him. As she asked him to go into the bathroom, take a bath and have breakfast before sitting down to watch TV, Janice came to sit quietly beside his brother and waited for what to do. If Jesam obeyed, he would too. He walked in the shadow of his big brother. Jesam shook his head and told Komomoh he wanted to watch cartoon and at that particular time. Komomoh said 'no', walked over to the TV and switched it off.

"You are not my mother, why should you tell me what to do?" he snapped. Komomoh was so shocked by the confrontation; she smacked Jesam on the cheek. It wasn't a hard hit. Jesam clutched his cheek and wailed. Keyu had left earlier for his office and no one was home with them, but Jesam cried with all his might and cried all through the day. He refused to eat or do anything Komomoh asked him. She was tempted to call Keyu and make a report but thought she could handle the situation. She tried to talk to Jesam, even pet him. She apologised and then got very upset with him. Nothing worked. Immediately their father returned from work, the boys reported their new mother, exaggerating about how hard she hit Jesam. Though Keyu rebuked them for not obeying their mother, it was half-hearted. He encouraged them to eat with him and they did. It was after the meal, in the safe confines of their room, Keyu requested 'Mom' never to touch his boys again.

Part of the duty of a mother is to spank.

It may sound hard and callous to some but it is scriptural. The Bible says that a good child is the pride of his father but a bad child is pain to the mother (paraphrasing). And foolishness is in the heart of a child but the rod of correction drives it far from him. If she's your wife and the new mother of your children, then let her do her duty. Don't get me wrong. There is what is called 'Wicked Stepmother'. They exist and I believe they do. And in your own best interest and that of your children, be wary about wicked stepmothers but this should be the exception and not the norm. Don't classify all women who are in this situation to be wicked. She may genuinely want to discipline and not punish. Children need discipline and you are not always there to do it. Don't make them feel she hates them and that you are the one that loves them. Allow her to raise her new children. Remember it's not easy on her. She will still feel those children have not forgotten their mother. She will need to know their and your acceptance in return. She needs to feel and know she is not second to the real. She needs to feel your love and that of the children.

Having said that, please I'll have you know that I refer to the woman after your heart. The woman who truly loves you and wants the best for you. Jesus asked Peter 'do you love me? Feed my sheep' Watch her closely and be sure she's real and fair and truly loves you before you thrust your children into her hands. And listen to your children. Watch their eyes and read their lips when they talk to you. Otherwise, I fully agree with the standing order.

WISDOM FOR MEN

OVER MY DEAD BODY

"CALABAR MEN ARE PROUD and lazy" Kojo said under his breath and sighed.

"Not all of them, my husband" Agbo replied, looking at him pleadingly. Cynthia sat at the edge of her seat, her large, lovely eyes pooling with tears. She prayed silently that God would soften her father's heart.

"I won't give my consent. You and your daughter can go and do whatever you like" he stood up.

"But Daddy, I…" Cynthia jumped to her feet.

"I will not have you marry a Calabar man that will not appreciate your worth and will just boast about foolishly. And I will not discuss this again" Kojo stomped out of the room.

"Mummy?" Cynthia burst into tears. "What is wrong with Okokon? He is one of the most blessed man on earth, very nice and caring and everything" she sobbed.

"I don't know for your father o. frankly, I will just advise you to find someone else, if you can" Agbo shrugged sadly.

"Hey, Mummy, hey…" Cynthia dried her tears angrily. "You will find husband for me o because I am tired of all this". She remembered what their father had said two years earlier when she came home with Nnaji. There was absolutely nothing to hold against him except that her father had not 'received' him. He needed the Holy Spirit to convince him first and refused the union because God did not speak.

Five months later, Cynthia met Jonathan, a young oil worker from Delta state. He was her dream come true. After thinking she would not be able to get over her loss of Okokon, he was hope renewed. She called him 'second chance' and told him God was giving her just that with him. She told her mother right away about the relationship. Contrary to what she expected, her mother was tense.

"Your father will not approve" Agbo said sorrowfully.

"Why not?" Cynthia chuckled. "Delta people are not lazy are they?" she said saucily but to her utter shock, her father refused even more bluntly than before.

"His people are our people's worst enemies. They fight us over boundaries and everything that goes with it. I will not sit down here and drink wine from an Urhobo's man's cup" Kojo said with a note of finality. He listened to the evening news calmly in the grave silence that ensued from his short speech.

Cynthia refused to take his word but after fighting over the issue for six months, gave up. Jonathan walked away with his heart broken.

"My father is making me choose between him and the man I will marry" she confided to one of her friends, Ada.

"Ignore him" her friend advised. "You are twenty–eight already. Will your father marry you? My father was like that too. After I watched Roots and saw the way the father ruined his daughter's life by refusing to allow her marry a half-caste, I changed my mind. The man said the half-caste is too white to be a black and too black to be a white. Can you imagine?"

"What has that got to do with anything?"

"He said the girl would be like an outcast married to a man like that. The blacks will not accept them, neither will the whites but I don't agree. The girl died an old maid" Ada hissed. "God forbid. My father too was carrying on about who to marry, said my Fidelis was an outcast. He didn't attend our wedding but today, everybody's enjoying"

So when Cynthia met Akin, she was determined to keep him. Akin was a lecturer in the Ogun State University and an Ijebu indigene. They courted for three months before Cynthia went ahead to tell her father.

"Over my dead body!" Kojo exclaimed. "Ijebu? Do you know what you are talking about? I could even tolerate the Calabar man or that Urhobo man but Ijebus are my own personal enemy. When I was in the army, it was an Ijebu man that set me up and I was disgraced out" he exclaimed. Cynthia had heard the story several times. "It was another Ijebu woman that poisoned my mother when we lived in Ebute-metta in Lagos. One other Ijebu boy married the first girl I wanted to marry before I met your mother. He actually came by and stole her from me! Ijebu, never!" Kojo said harshly.

"Then who should I marry, Daddy" Cynthia wailed.

"Are Ijaw boys finished on this earth?" Kojo asked saucily. "You haven't seen a husband o. I don't even want to see that boy in my house!"

When Cynthia tried to break up with Akin, hoping a right Ijaw man would come along; he bluntly refused and told her to pray for her father.

"I will pray that he changes his mind. You are my wife, that one I know" Akin insisted.

While still maintaining his stand on the issue after six months, Kojo had a grisly accident and was hospitalised. Akin and Cynthia decided to continue with plans for their wedding, leaving Kojo completely out of the preparations. The surgery performed on him developed complications and sadly Kojo died three months after the auto accident, and several operation procedures. Till his death, he insisted that Cynthia would marry an Ijebu man over his dead body. The family mourned him for three months after which Akin and Cynthia got married in a quiet ceremony.

Don't kill yourself, I beg you. There are a lot more things to life than insisting on living another person's life for her or him. You are a father mainly to guide, direct and advice. I do agree that parents should be respected for their opinion in the choice of a life partner. An adage says that what a child climbs the tree and not see, an old man seats under the tree and sees clearly. But still, you have to give your child space as an adult to make his choices. Destiny is a choice. You may not even have an accident and die, that happens in rare cases but what if you don't die, and refuse to attend their wedding, and refuse to share in their joy, and disown them and cause sorrow for all concerned parties, most including yourself, and they make it together. Before your very eyes, your greatest fear concerning them refuses to materialize, they have beautiful children (and you have banned them from your house), and progress in their lives? What if things work out for them, without you? It's just not worth losing sleep over. Pray for them, advise them. If you have strong reasons to doubt, let them know but don't hook their relationship with you on their relationship with another. You knew them before the spouse came along.

WISDOM FOR MEN

SHE'S DISTRACTED, WHAT DO I DO?

WHEN HE WALKED IN through the door, there was a lull all around. It was unusual and Greg called out to find out if anyone was home. The walls and furniture responded to his call. He dropped his briefcase on the dining table and pulled on his tie. He walked first into the kitchen and poured a glass of cold water for himself. As he drank he walked into the room to finish his undressing. He was famished. Where was his wife for Chrissakes! He switched on the TV and browsed through all the channels of the DSTV and finally settled for channel 67, animal planet. Amazing animal videos was on and much as he loved to watch and amuse himself, his mind was distracted tonight. His stomach rumbled again in angry indictment. He pulled himself up and strolled back into the kitchen. The cooker was clean and clear. The sink area was spotless. He checked the kitchen table; the rack was neatly stacked with clean crockery. A cooler sat beside the rack. He opened it and to his great relief found steaming coconut rice and fried turkey inside. He picked a plate and dished the food for himself, still wondering where Salewa was. She knew he was due back and she was nowhere to be found. And she'd left the front door open. Suddenly panic gripped him, could she have left the house in an emergency? Her phone rang several times before she picked it, and then with a slur apologised and told him she was in the neighbourhood and would soon be home. Briskly he looked for and found coleslaw in the freezer and angrily settled down to a meal. He had just returned from a weeklong trip and she was not there for him. What a callous thing to do, to keep food for him in a cooler and take a stroll in the neighbourhood when he had been longing so much to be back and to see her. He had recently been noticing the attitudes, telltale signs of lack of commitment or boredom. She took little interest in the house and often stayed late in her chemist, sometimes coming home later than him. Several times she forgot to pick up their four-year old daughter from school and end up having the teacher call him to come. Recently also, he noticed she complained about everything. She was tired of her business she said. She wanted a paid job with regular hours. Then she said she wanted to go into the Dubai business her friend was in to. She hated being married to a civil servant she complained and asked him to try and get a job with a private organisation or set up his own civil engineering firm. Then she got personal. She hated men with athlete's foot like he had. She hated the hair in his armpit and asked him to shave. She hated the way they made love, and said she always had. Her needs became endless and irritating and Greg began to wonder if she was seeing someone else. She was restless around the house and forgot things easily. It was so bad, their sixth wedding anniversary came and she didn't remember until the evening when he returned from a site he was inspecting and gave her a gift.

Greg felt a strange foreboding, and struggled to shake it off. If there was someone else, he guessed he would know but why would Salewa cheat? He had always thought everything was great between them. At one point in their relationship, he had even thought she loved him too much.

When she returned that fateful night, he confronted her about her behaviour and got the shock of his life when she told him, "I'm just tired of this marriage".

What happened to the woman you married? This is a question I would love to ask Father Adam when we get to heaven. Where were you when she started 'getting distracted'? Having chats with the enemy and the neighbors and all sorts of company, keeping late nights and leaving your food to cool off in a cooler. Please search your soul. Remember what your beginning was like. When she was showing all the love and attention what were you doing? Busy piling your degrees? Or building your business empire? Or getting the promotions in your office? Pursuing political ambitions? Where were you? She may not be cheating but just trying to get your attention. She may also just be spoiling for a fight so you'll know she's been neglected. And if you can boldly say you were there for her, then probably she's cheating! And that is another problem entirely. Why would your woman need the attention of another man? Have you been taking care of her? Don't get blinded by fury about this question. Women have deep sexual needs that need to be met. Your intercourse should not end when you climax. What happens after? What happened before? Spice up your marriage with good sex. Let her leave your arms smiling and hugging her body. And you can start right away. Please pay attention to her needs. Some women are sterilized units. Hygiene is paramount to them; indulge your wife if she's like that. Be good to her. Say nice things to her and about her. Court her. Your marriage is important, watch over it. God help you too. Amen.

WISDOM FOR MEN

HOME ALONE

PAUL LOOKED ROUND THE house, touching surfaces and feeling textures. It was truly over, he thought warily. It was a sad-joy feeling. Sad for being home alone; joy for being free. Even though he didn't wholly see how that freedom would help him yet. She was quite gone. Quite. Today they had appeared in court for the last time. She had worn a red skirt suit that flared her fair complexion. He noticed she had changed her hair colour to blonde. To provoke him, he was certain. He loved her natural black hair but over the years he had seen all sorts on her head from gold to red, to white and blonde. He hated the white and the blonde most. A fair-complexion like hers was loud enough and he didn't like loud women. Several times his mother had asked him the one-word question, why? He knew what she meant but he had never allowed her to elaborate and he had never given her a reply. Wasn't that one of the antidotes for a successful marriage but now it was over, he guessed it was time to look at the whys. Where did who go wrong and how; what could have been done or otherwise.

They'd been separated throughout all the court procedure months. It had given him a chance to sample what it would be like when she was finally gone. But today, with the final verdict in, it felt terribly different. Terribly lonely. She had accused him of being arrogant and rude. Hah! His sins were minuscule compared to hers but she took the 'attack is the best form of defense' approach. She shouted 'foul' before he even realized there was a fight. Hadn't pastor told him not to look for blames? But how would he, could he move on without looking back, just once in a while? His mother had asked to come over and spend the night, he said NO! Please. She would look for every way to make him happy. He wasn't happy. He didn't want to be happy. His life was in shambles.

"It's unbelievable she's finally gone" Paul muttered and slumped into a chair, his voice sounded many miles away, echoing in his head. He swallowed and looked round the house, stripped of her beauty. Her presence. Paula was a beauty. She had presence. Somehow he was grateful she'd picked all her stuff out before today. He couldn't have been able to look at her portraits on his wall, her scent, though still lingered was faint now.

Oh God! He heaved a heavy sigh and thought he would cry but he was beyond that. He hoped he was. Who was it that told him a good cry was good? He couldn't remember, couldn't put his mind out to anything right now. Paulina too was gone. Lovely girl with her mother's… everything! Fair skin, large eyes, oval face, long black hair, that dark mole just above the corner of her upper lip, on the left side… that lovely spot! And the gap tooth. He couldn't forget sliding his tongue in between it. No, I can't do this to myself. He jumped to his feet and strolled resolutely to the bedroom. Too many memories. He walked over to the kitchen and sat on the low stool there, the only furniture in the kitchen. She'd taken everything. He was empty, lonely. He should be hungry but who would think of hunger on a day like this. Still his stomach rumbled. Go get a burger, it sang. You are good to go for fast foods now! It teased him. Paula had been a great cook. Unlike most sophisticated high-class girls, she hated eating out. In fact, that was one of the many things that thrilled him about her. Too many things thrilled him about her. Tears pooled in his eyes. May be he should give in to it. Pastor had wanted to come and stay with him but not tonight, tomorrow, maybe. May be he shouldn't have allowed her to divorce him. Maybe he should have fought to keep her, but…

Paulina's face would forever haunt him. The fact that she may not have been his was overwhelming. He had waited and prayed so long for her and when she'd come along, it had been his dream come through. He decided he wanted to think about Paulina. She was balm to his aches. For the four years he had her, he was grateful to God. Even if she wasn't his, he hadn't had the confidence to do the DNA for fear of what it would produce, better to keep speculating but even then, if she wasn't his, he would always love her. She was his sunshine.

"I'll never marry again" he spoke aloud. But even as he said it, his body told him otherwise. Paula had roused feelings he never imagined existed. He hadn't been a virgin when he married her either. Good God, take these thoughts away from me, a voice moaned from within. He didn't recognize it as his.

"I will walk backwards to where it all began from. To the night I caught her with another man in my bedroom, to the moment she asked for a divorce while I stood watching her... with another man. I will forgive her, and work at forgetting. I will move on and forget tonight. Stripped, bared and cheated"

When he opened his eyes, he was back in his bedroom, on that night, seeing Paula in another man's arms and telling him she wanted a divorce, telling him Paulina wasn't his after all.

Back to the beginning.

He gave himself up to the privilege of tears.

At one point in every man's life, there is that need to reflect and to make amends. This is a very sad story but every man experiences a rape of justice in one aspect or the other of their lives. It could be marital, financial, career-wise, even at some spiritual stratum, you feel used, cheated. It's time to walk back to that point where you first believed. To go back to that point where things went really wrong and straighten it. Forgiveness does that for you. It makes the crooked path straight and brightens your path. Don't look at the pain but at the gain. If she must go, let her go but move on also. If that good thing you thought you had; that job, that woman, that expectation, that child, that contract; takes a leap and leaves you behind, move on. It will get better. You will make it, in Jesus' name. Amen.

WISDOM FOR MEN

HEY, GOOD LOOKING

ASHI'S WIFE ATIM WAS the ideal woman every man wanted. She was a slim, tall, dark-skinned bundle of beauty with a superior figure. Anything she wore fitted her as though she was in the designer's thoughts when the design was being conceived. The third in a family of five and the only girl, she had always been the apple of everyone's eyes. She had the best education available in the country and after graduating in business administration from the university of Lagos, had gone ahead to do her masters degree in public speaking in America. It was while there she met Ashi who had just begun to practice his medicine. The relationship was an instant hit and they'd gotten married almost immediately; roughly four months after they set eyes on each other for the first time. Ashi worked three jobs seven days a week. Atim worked two, six days a week and in the midst of it, they had two lovely daughters. Being a working mother was quite challenging but Atim was a bulldozer in the face of challenges. Together and with twenty years of hard work, they were back home to settle down. Ashi set up a clinic in Calabar to practice his gynaecology. Atim pooled her years of experience together co-hosting a TV game show, and started one on the local TV. It was an instant hit.

When weighed, Ashi was more of a success financially, even though he was hardly seen except by his patients, but Atim was on screen. Within the first six months of the game show, she had spread her tentacles and was on five TV stations and negotiating with four more. Her success was compound. By the end of the first year, she had sponsors from more than ten leading companies ranging from communications and banking to household and oil & gas. She had her personal wardrobe and beauty consultants and was fast working towards setting up her own studio.

On the home front, she insisted on being a wife and mother. Including the days she did her recordings, she maintained a sane atmosphere; making sure she cooked all meals for her family. Their two daughters she had insisted returned home with them aged fifteen and ten were placed in boarding schools and whenever they were home took part in being valuable. To discipline herself, Atim refused the services of a helper around the house. To many who were close to her, she became a case study.

Late one evening, Ashi returned late from work and found his wife crying on the sofa in the living room of their quaint four-bedroom duplex. It had been a particularly difficult day for him with two deliveries, one a complicated multiple birth, and one D&C for a young woman whose careless abortion trial had left her almost dead by the time she was rushed into his clinic. Besides it was his family planning day and he had been on his feet for almost ten hours straight by the time he got home. He was dead on his feet and wanted to head straight to bed after a good meal. The first thing he noticed when he walked in was that the lights were out in the guest sitting room downstairs. That was strange because she always left it on till he was in. He took the stairs two at a time and found her whimpering into a handkerchief. As she normally did, she was ready for his homecoming. She was bathed and fresh and spotting a clean floral house-wear. Even in the simple attire, she looked exotic.

He dropped his office bag on the floor carelessly and half-ran to her. The house was otherwise quiet as the girls were away in school.

"Sweetheart" he dropped to his knees before her, his fatigue completely gone, replaced with apprehension. "What's the matter?"

She sniffed and hugged him tight.

"Tell me" he huffed into the hollow of her neck.

"I'm going to have a baby!" she said. "I can't believe it. I'm still on contraceptives for God's sake" she sniffed, searching his face. How could this be? She was forty-two hadn't had a baby in ten years and didn't plan on having one. This would totally disrupt her life. Her husband would hate her for this... this mistake.

He burst into laughter to her disbelief.

"Great!" he slumped back, looking at her with admiration. "I'm going to be a father, again" he threw his arms above his head and laughed. She blew her nose into the handkerchief, astonished.

"You're not mad?" she asked looking at him. He shook his head; hunger and fatigue had now flown out of the window. He had a sweet feeling in his stomach. "This is going to change our lives" she gasped, "A baby!"

"A blessing" he replied.

"God, I love you" she jumped on his neck and kissed him soundly.

How will it be with you or how has it been, two months, two years or twenty years after marriage. Where are the romance and the love? Contentment is paramount in every marriage and it comes by staying together, doing things together, planning and working together. When there are mistakes, do you heap the 'coal' on your partner's head? Or see the brighter side of the dull sky. We are bound to change over the years. Our children, our careers and the people we meet change and tend to change us but as we grow together, do we also grow apart? Love is a man's duty around the house and the show of it brings tremendous results. Don't say 'let her submit first, and then I will love her'. That is a coward's statement. Show love, care and understanding and see what you'll get. Don't assume that your wife is one of those women who will take advantage of your kindness and show of love. And even if she did it before, forgive, forget and give her chance after chance to be the woman you want her to be. Remember you are also not perfect and even if you are before her, what about in the sight of God who asked you to love her as He loves you. Loving your wife does not mean you are weak. Coming home early to your wife does not mean she'll become careless. Encourage your woman to have a vision and a purpose and work towards helping her actualise it. When the success comes, you'll be the first to reap. Determine not to follow statusquo. Apologise when you're wrong.

Love your woman.

WISDOM FOR MEN

ANOTHER PIECE OF FURNITURE, PLEASE!

UCHENNA'S WEDDING CEREMONY WAS just as he had seen it turn out to be. It was a society wedding. He had not worked in Holland for four years for nothing, saving every kobo he earned. He wasn't a spendthrift, far from it. Instead, he was a careful planner. Everything he did was according to his budget. So far, so good. When his mother had pestered him about marriage previously, he'd asked her to forget it. When it was time, he would seek her out. He had taken up the business challenge in Holland and invested four years of his life into it. A year before he returned, he'd called his mother.

"I need a wife" he said. She laughed and screamed, thanking him for finally talking about it.

"You want me to find one for you?" she asked, knowing his reply.

"A good girl, from a good family. And she must be born again" he said emphatically.

"No problem. No problem. O Chineke m o!" she had said jubilantly.

"Tell Chuks to send her picture through my email address when you find someone" he told her. She had hurriedly hung up. She knew whom she wanted for her son. Ihunna was the daughter of her very good friend. A very good and well brought up girl. And she loved God. She had a melodious voice too and sang in the choir of her church. Besides, she already had admission in the university. Uchenna would be pleased with that. She knew her son well. Mama Uchenna had been planning it for a long time but knew she couldn't jump on her son like that. She would wait for a few days, maybe a week and then give Chukwuka Ihunna's pictures. She was a very fair and beautiful girl.

When Uchenna opened the pictures of the Ihunna, he had been delighted. She had also sent a mail, a shy mail to her, introducing herself and asking about him. For six months they chatted and he grew to like her. At Christmas, he met her for the first time and confirmed all he had assumed. She was good for him. A man of action, he started the marriage rites before he went back. He had a few months left according to his plans to return and he would celebrate his return home with his traditional and church wedding.

Everything went as planned. Uchenna, who was into furniture business, was tremendously successful. He had built for himself a niche that was hard to rival, stretching his empire from Onitsha, Aba and Owerri to Portharcourt, Enugu and Lagos. Through all his years abroad, his business sailed smoothly, a feat few could achieve. Uchenna was by all standards, a highly principled and successful man, and it was this approach that had worked so perfectly in the business front that he brought home. He ruled his hand with an iron fist. He believed in schedules and was opposed to disorder. His home was governed like a military camp, his two brothers and all five dependants living with him in full awareness of the rituals.

When Ihunna stepped into her matrimonial home the first day, she felt like a new addition to the expensive furniture that graced the room, a showcase of Uchenna's business empire. She hated white furniture and that was what Uchenna's house basically comprised of. White rug! She noticed the lobby filled with shoes on her entrance and soon discovered why. She was just thinking of when would be right to broach the topic of changing the entire interior when he called the whole household together, after dinner. Ihunna counted the number of mouths she'd just inherited on her first day at home. Seven adults; four men and three women. She wanted to laugh. This indeed was marriage. Well, everyone was in for this one.

"I called this meeting to introduce my wife whom you all already know anyway but to formally hand over the house to her" Uchenna started in his characteristic way of doing things. All was properly planned. He had everything in perspective. "Chukwuka, or Chuks if you like, is my junior brother, and Obinna is my other junior brother". Ihunna had met them both at the family house. "Uzo and Nneka are my cousins" the two girls smiled at Ihunna. She did not return the enthusiasm. "Godwin is an apprentice". Ihunna gasped, apprentice in the house? "Azuka is a friend's cousin". All the while, Uchenna did not notice his new wife's stance. He went ahead to tell them all things would remain as usual. Everyone should go about their duties and give his respect they would accord him. Everyone welcomed the new madam and retired.

Safe in the confines of their bedroom, after consummating their union, Ihunna shyly asked her husband to hear out her comments about the evening's meeting.

"I cannot cope with seven adults in the house; let everyone go, except your two brothers." She started.

"My dear…"

"Please let me finish so I won't forget" she said softly. He shrugged. "I need to redecorate the whole house. The furniture and draperies are too white and not realistic for maintenance purposes. I will do all my cooking and cleaning myself, please so that if anyone wants to give me stress, I can send them easily back to where they are coming from. Last but not the least is that I can't afford more than a week of grace for the changes to take place. That's all I have to say, my husband. Please indulge me so that we will enjoy this marriage", she sighed. Uchenna kept quiet for what seemed like ages, trying his best to control his anger.

"This is my house, Ihunna. And you are my wife, and fine if things don't suit you well right now, I understand. But to start sending people out and making all those drastic changes don't suit me. I am a very logical person and I like to plan and right now, all those things you suggested don't fit into my plan. Try and understand that, please" he said slowly to conceal his irritation. She waited him out and when she realised he had finished, smiled but her retort only mirrored the war she was about to declare.

"Well, my husband, that was well said, but remember, I am your wife, not an additional piece of furniture in your house"

She turned her back and within minutes, slept off. Uchenna, fuming in the dark room, half-smiled. This was war, he thought, and began to plan his strategy.

As soon as you get married, two becomes one. Many times, that arithmetic eludes men. Especially if he is already established and comfortable. I know a man who had restrictions on the use of his car. This can't be right. Don't look on her as another piece of your acquisition; a milestone arrived at, a victory flag. Instead, she is a life partner, a soul mate. When you look at her, see a counsellor, a friend, a confidant and this is why it is good you connect with your wife properly before you plunge into marriage. Even if the marriage was 'arranged' scratch the surface, and learn to plan together; it is a more difficult task but one that should be accomplished. The point is whether you found yourselves or were introduced; whether you courted for a month or a year, if you want to be open, you will be. If you want to plan together, you can even if ten thousand miles separate you. Otherwise, you will be caught in a web and an entanglement you probably aren't prepared for. The first step if you find yourself in this dilemma is to start to change your mindset. She is not another trophy won. Involve her in your decision-making tasks. There are frankly some issues a woman need not know of before it matures or doubt and fear may make her terminate it (be sensitive) but issues that concern your home concerns her primarily too. Involve her. The second step is to be patient with her. Don't rush and plan for war. The home is meant to be a haven of comfort not a battlefield. If you understand this, and accept it, you may slow down on your war strategies. A third step is to draw her closer to you, lead by example and love and make it clear to her that you are the man and the head of the family. Whatever decision you make in your home is subject to your final ratification. One other thing to do is to be ready to compromise. If she wants five things, find a level ground and indulge her some. It makes her realise that you have no personal grudge against her and that you are not selfish. It also helps her understand you are not callous and insensitive to her desires. May God help you along.

WISDOM FOR MEN

BETWEEN YOU AND HER

THE FRONT GATE OPENED with its usual irritating scratch on the hinges and Tope peeped out of the window above the laundry room where she was ironing Soji's clothes. The slight stretching of her neck was done more on impulse than she cared to admit. Especially since that cringe had almost become a part of day sounds around her. In her mind's eye, she saw the gate open and close, not so carefully, and one guest or the other strolled in. They had asked the paid staff to use the back gate to come in when they needed to. That way, Tope's neck would know less stretching. The design of the house had caused part of the problem. All the activity rooms stretched across the front gate: the laundry, the kitchen and the plant nursery. These were her work areas and though concealed from the front, she only needed to stretch to get a drift of who was walking the quarter kilometre to their home.

Today, Tope's body went rigid as she saw who approached. Soji's mother. Carrying a small raffia bag and trudging behind her was the little boy she usually came with. For that boy, she had a story to tell like she had for everyone she came across. The boy, according to her, had been abandoned as a ten-month old baby on her doorstep eight years earlier.

She had taken and cared for the child as her own. To Tope though, the boy looked thick-necked and more like fifteen.

"What does she want?" Tope muttered. She switched off the iron and hung her apron on the wall. "Your son is not home" she added as she checked her face in the wall mirror she regularly thanked God for having her hang on the wall. Her mother-in-law complained too often about her being too westernised for no just cause. Convenience had nothing to do with sophisticates! Her face in the mirror met with approval of the one looking at it. She snickered, drew in a breath and then went to the door. It would take another minute or two before they knocked. She hated this woman! Hate is ungodly her spirit chided. Oh strong dislike then, for the Christian vocabulary. Distaste. Abhor. And the latest word she learnt from Reader's Digest, Odium. Hm. Soji, come home now, I command you in Jesus' name she breathed the moment before the doorbell went. Mama usually kept her hand on it till someone got the door. She relished another second of peace and jerked the door open as Agatha, the housekeeper rushed in. Despite having a cook and housekeeper, Tope did a great deal of work around the house.

"Mama!" she greeted coolly as the older woman all but shoved her aside as she stepped in.

"New furniture again?" she gaped at Tope. The little boy released the raffia bag on the floor almost spilling its contents, and dropped into a single sofa as though he'd been trekking across the Sahara for days.

"Soji changed the colour last week" she said dryly.

"Is that why you refused to allow him send money to me last week?" she looked at Tope squarely. "You take the bags to the room" she looked at the boy, briskly dismissing him.

"Money is not Soji's problem and you know it. Even if he spent a million bucks on his furniture. Will you shower before you eat?" Tope changed the topic neatly.

"I know my way around here" Mama said seedily and went straight to the kitchen. She gave instructions to Agatha and Salome the cook; then went upstairs to take a bath. And so began Tope's hospitality to her mother-in-law. Over the years of her marriage to Soji, she had honed her skills of communicating with her. She had never gotten much help from her husband though his presence helped in distracting Mama. Ultimately, they would have an ugly fight and Mama would leave. It would usually happen when Soji, a senior staff of a leading oil company was off at work. Twice when Soji and his wife were out of the country on short term assignments, Mama had been invited over and had caused so much stress, Soji's boss had advised they not invite Mama over again.

Tope shrugged and went back to her ironing. She was a housewife, bound to receive guests on behalf of her husband and if the guest refused to cooperate with her, she let them be. And that was what she did till Soji returned in the early evening. She had refused to call him to hint about his mother's visit because it made no difference. He was very close to his mother and though they had been married for thirteen years, on many occasions, Soji sought and took his mother's advice, sometimes to her contrary views. Mama came and went as she liked and there was nothing she could do about that.

All through dinner, Mama chattered, something Soji hated after a long day at work but this was Mama not Tope. She talked about everything; from the last burial in the village to why she still worried he wasn't feeding well. Tope kept mute, studying a women's magazine as though she had an exam on it the following day. They all retired early, as soon as Soji took an excuse and went to bed.

"Why do you think Mama came?" Tope asked cautiously as they prepared to sleep.

"She needs money" Soji said shortly.

"Why didn't she call, instead of travelling all the way? And, you just gave her something two weeks ago"

"She said it finished"

"Finished. Soji dear, eighty thousand finished in two weeks, in fact last week because she's been calling since then... " her mouth drooped as she realised what she'd done. Lying blatantly about her mother-in-law not calling and then just saying the opposite. She had never been good at lying; especially to her husband.

"You didn't tell me she called" Soji said softly on a wedge of steel.

"I forgot" she sighed. "How much are you giving her?"

"As much as I see keen. I work for the money" he said stiffly.

"I work for you" she reiterated, and slid into his arms to sleep. No point arguing.

At about midnight, there was a knock on their door. Mama wanted to talk to her son. Though it had never happened before and Tope saw it as a calculated attempt to annoy her, she excused her husband and his mother and finished off her sleep on the sofa in the living room. She'd thought she could wait up but by the time she drifted off in sleep, Mama was still talking.

Mama stayed for two hellish weeks on that trip. On the day she was to leave, Salome called Tope aside and told her Mama had cooked a month's reserve of soups and instructed her not to serve Soji any other food apart from that. Sparks went off in Tope's head. She stomped out to the front of the house where Soji about to take Mama to the village, was stacking the boot of his Audi A6 Saloon car with Mama's things, while Mama stood by and fondly watched. In Tope's hand was a carton with neatly stacked bowls containing Mama's soups. She was fuming, something she rarely did.

"You have forgotten this, Mama" she said and dumped the carton in the boot.

"What is this?" Soji asked, surprised by her demeanour.

"Your mother's soup" Tope said tartly.

"Soup!" Mama and Soji quizzed together. "Mama you cooked soup to take?" Soji asked.

"This your wife is a very foolish woman. Take that soup back before I curse you" Mama said angrily.

"What is going on here?" Soji spat, looking at Tope.

"Mama cooked soup for you as though we in this house don't know how to cook. What is the meaning of that?"

"What is the meaning of my mother cooked soup? Is it not to help you?" he asked. Tope wanted to counter him with a question of her own, Are you daft?

"Not when I didn't ask for the help. Not when I didn't know she was helping me" Tope said heatedly. "Can you imagine Salome just told me now" she yelled. She'd had about enough.

"Why are you so angry" Soji looked at her and then Mama.

"I wonder o, my son. As if I want to poison you or what. Can you see this is how she treats me" Mama said feebly.

"Well, what's your problem? Please take the soup back" Soji said.

"Take the soup back? Oh, please" Tope stretched every word.

"Well, this is between you and Mama" Soji started to move away, "when you are finished let me know but remember I still have to come back today"

Tope's hand shot out from Mars and pulled him back violently, stunning all of them.

"No, this is between you and her. I've taken this for long enough" she rushed back into the house, sobbing as she went. She had never dragged him like that before and she still couldn't help imagining the repercussion. She was in for it. She heard him bark her name a couple of times ordering her to come back but she only slammed shut and lock the door to her bedroom behind her. Alone, she wiped her face and burst into laughter.

'You're in trouble now with him' she thought aloud. 'That's what she's always wanted. She wins'.

It is important as the man of the house to stand in the gap between your wife and your family. You brought her to them and it is your responsibility to ensure cordiality and sanity between them. Don't throw your wife to the dogs, forgiving me here that I use such an idiom. But when there is trouble between her and your family, you are the one that has to balance things up. It's not the time to start taking sides and if you must, there is no controversy about whose side you should take – your wife's. After all, she's the better half of you. Your mother had the final say about your diet the day before your marriage, after that, she is ex-officio. Respect her and keep her where she belongs. The marriage vows were taken by husband and wife with no additions. By not keeping your mother or father or any other family member where they belong as extended members of your family, you are simply opening yourself up for disrespect from them because if they cuss at your wife, the message is for you. If they maltreat and backstab your wife, they are also rejoicing you are getting the message. If they truly love you, they'll treat your woman with love and respect. Don't turn away, face it. Let decisions about your welfare stay between you and your wife.

God is still on the throne and He remembers His own.

WISDOM *for* WOMEN

Pr 4:7 Wisdom is the principal thing; Therefore get wisdom. And in all your getting, get understanding.

Dedicated to my mother:
Mrs. A. T. Ifaturoti
A wise woman, a virtuous woman

CONTENTS

WISDOM FOR WOMEN

WHEN HE RAISES HIS HAND!

Sumbo received the slap with shock!

She wasn't sure which of the options brought her to her knees; either the weight of his massive hand, the impact of the slap or the shock from the action. One thing was sure though; the tears that sprang to her eyes.

Her initial feeling of shock was quickly turned to fear but when she summoned enough courage to look into his eyes, the fear turned to outrage. He looked almost as confused as her.

How dare he?

This was it, she thought. I will not condone this. Once it starts, it will never stop. That was the advice she'd been given. 'Don't ever allow him to raise his hand on you. Once he does it the first time, you're in trouble'.

Sumbo picked herself up with the newly acquired zeal.

Femi speechlessly took a step away from her. She moved to her wardrobe and pulled out an overnight bag. Tonight she would sleep in Erebi's house; tomorrow, she would contact her lawyer and take things as they unfold from there.

"What are you doing?" Femi's voice shook slightly.

Why talk to a foolish wife-batterer, a brute?

She continued what she was doing, ignoring him. She pulled a denim skirt, two tank tops, and a trouser suit for work the following day, office shoes, bag, jewellery and accessories. A casual dress followed into the bag and a couple of under wears.

"You can't do what you're thinking" Femi sounded alarmed. "Please".

"Watch me"

What did he think he was doing when he raised his barbaric hand? This is it.

This is the end.

Shi ke na!

Interestingly, there was hardly any mention of wife beating in the scriptures. Have you ever wondered why? I have. Could it be that the women in the days of the scriptures were so serene and submissive and the men were so understanding and nice that there was no need for battering? Or wife beating was not worth mentioning? Or it was so concealed that the leaders of the church were not aware? Whatever the case, it is of increasing concern to the Pentecostal leaders today. On TBN, a woman of God quoted that in today's America, one of four women is suffering from battering. That is an alarming fraction. I am concerned, and every Godly woman should be too whether they are victims or not.

Let's take a close look:

Men hit their wives for one or more of these among other reasons:

▫ To establish his authority. Every woman should remember that God placed the staff of leadership in the hands of the man. Don't allow your man to HAVE to establish his authority over you, especially in such a way**. There are ways to go about it, *be soft spoken   *talk to him when he's in a good mood *speak politely and positively *discover your husband's style. The list is endless.

** (Other ways which include 'the silent treatment'; 'psychological battery' will be treated some other time)

⊡ To calm hysterics. Women have a lot of pressure in their lives. From struggling with maintaining a good look to the stress of having OR NOT having children, keeping their jobs and businesses, house work, giving attention to husband, children, friends, in-law, and generally serving HER whole world, it can get really tedious. A woman's anger and hysterics though not justified should never be CALMED with a slap or more. It is UNFAIR. However, a woman should prayerfully wear the pressures off. Do the things you enjoy and concentrate more on being happy and content than carrying the frustration out on others, especially your husband.

⊡ To punish her behaviour. Men who hurt their wives because of her foul or wrong behaviour are only trying to tell the world they are less MEN. If you could win her the first time to marry her, you can win her again and again without force. No one is perfect and it is unfair again to punish an adult as though a child. Pray for this man but be sure you also put in some effort into avoiding what irritates him most.

⊡ His wife wants him to do it. Some women are SICK enough to believe that when he hits them, he loves them. Others use it as a means of acquiring gifts. "Each time he beats me up, he apologises with gold!" So they provoke him into raising his hand. Well, well I warn you sister, mend your thoughts. You may soon run out of gifts because he may still continue hitting you when he's broke. Mend your ways.

The bottom line as Christian women is to remember Eph.5: 22-24 and to strive prayerfully to stick to every word of it. May God help us all.
Amen.

WISDOM FOR WOMEN

WHAT DO MEN REALLY WANT?

Everyone thought Chinedu had a great wife. Ngozi, his wife was sweet to behold. Though a mother of two adorable children, she was prim and tight! She was tall, slim and with cream chocolate colour, a beauty. Her oval shaped eyes, slim, pointed nose and full lips balanced well on her smooth face. Her hair, usually worn naturally (without attachments) was long, dark and silky. Physically, Ngozi always attracted a second glance. Even from fellow women.

To complement her beauty, Ngozi had a sweet outward approach. She took compliments with humility, and took care of her home, as every woman should. Her children, ages 8 and 6 appeared neat and well-spoken in public. They were courteous at all times and never played rough or misbehaved as most children did. Looking at Ngozi, one naturally concluded she was blessed. To make family life easy for her, she had chosen the teaching profession and had a fine job as a University lecturer. It afforded her time to take care of her life and concerns.

When Chinedu announced at Workers' meeting in church, in confession; that he had indeed filed for a divorce, everyone gasped in shock. And many asked the same question – WHAT MORE DOES HE WANT? He was a devoted father, hardworking and seemed enough like a family man.

"Had that girl not done enough?"

"I ate in her house once, she is a great cook?"

"Her in-laws adore her. It couldn't be them"

Some even dared to voice the abominable…

"Could it be another woman outside?"

"Maybe she's not performing in bed…HAAAA?"

"Should a man divorce because of sexual dissatisfaction?"

"Maybe she was unfaithful"

The gossip was endless. It was so bad, it became a concern to the pastorate and the pastor had to pay Chinedu a private visit. Some questions needed to be answered.

The answers that came from Chinedu shocked all that heard.

Yes, Ngozi was very beautiful, attractive. A fantastic and faithful lover. Sex was not the problem.

Yes, Ngozi was a good home maker. She was a great cook. She cleaned the house and kept things in order.

Yes, Ngozi was a humble in-law. She respected Chinedu's family and made sure they were always comfortable around their son.

Yes, Ngozi was a great mother. She gave adequate time to the care of her children. She fed them with good food, bought quality clothes for them, saw that they were concentrating in school and made sure all round they were given the best of all their needs.

No, Ngozi was not a good wife to her husband. She criticized his every business and financial move. She nagged endlessly even when he has apologized for wrong done to her. She unendingly compared him to other men especially his colleagues in business (apparently, Chinedu had not really succeeded as well as his mates). She expressed regret for marrying him on a daily basis.

All these made it hard for him to see all the other good in her.

She was the sweetest friend, daughter, sister, and mother but as a wife, she was none.

Is this possible? I hear a sister ask. My reply is 'Search Me!'

I took a small poll and asked a number of women and men what the MEN really want.

Women said:

Beautiful appearance

Good food

Respect

Sex

Men said:

Respect

Sex, (as much as they want)

Submission

Encouragement and praise

Beautiful appearance

God said:

As unto the Lord! (Ephesians 5)

HOLD ON! APOLOGIES FIRST!!

WHEN ALERO WHISPERED THAT Temisan had not eaten her food for three days, everyone gasped. How can't you cook for your husband for THREE DAYS! It wasn't that she hadn't cooked. She did cook but he was upset with her and that was his way of expressing anger. Alero was advised that it wasn't the best and she had to apologise and make up for the sake of peace. It seemed such a hard thing for her to do but she pulled herself together, went on her knees before her husband and offered him his favourite food. Her friends had advised her not to bring up the issue that caused the problem in the first instance.

"Whatever I did or said in the first place, I'm sorry. Please forgive me" Alero said humbly.

"Oh, so you have now realized your mistake, uhn?" he snickered. "You think you can be stubborn with me? I wonder what they teach you in your women meeting. You know me; I can do without your food forever. Once I eat two slices of bread, a can of juice. I'm okay. I was just waiting for the day you will come to your senses. I don't have any problem…" he went on and on and on.

Alero remained on her knees, staring at her, struggling with the urge to rise up and walk off. He had been the one who offended. Why are men like this? She thought. She blanked him out knowing that was the only way she could pull this through. Finally, he kept quiet.

Alero said, "I'm sorry. Please forgive me"

"It's alright. What choice do I have?"

"Thank you" she said quietly, seething.

Temisan ate the food with relish. In his heart of hearts, he had missed her cooking but 'one had to teach these women a lesson at times'.

The next time they had a major disagreement, Temisan again refused to eat. He bought a carton of canned juice and assorted biscuits and fed himself with junk. After a week of no improvement, he started coming home with fast foods. Mostly fried rice and spaghetti. Alero determined in her mind to frustrate him and stop the stupid childish behaviour.

A week after the problem started, they were still keeping malice around the house. Alero was adamant. She was not going to budge so that Temisan's madness will stop.

The phone rang and there was an important message concerning a contract they had been praying about for months. Alero was excited. As soon as Temisan walked in she rushed outside to welcome him.

"Oh welcome" she greeted. "The people…"

"If you're not going to apologise for your foolishness, get out of my way!" Temisan snapped.

"You don't even know what I want to say. It's good…"

"I don't care, you hear" he shouted at the top of his voice and stomped into the house.

"Who will lose?" Alero hissed and went back into the house.

Two more days passed.

Alero knew they will both lose if that contract was lost so she tried to talk to her husband about it. When he still refused to give her audience, she wrote the message on a piece of paper and left it in his briefcase. That evening when Temisan came back from work, he was in a very bad mood.

"You see!" he yelled. "Did I marry a wife or a witch? They told you to convey an important message but your pride stood in the way" he ranted.

"What are you talking about?"

"The contract! I'm talking about the contract. We lost it. You hear?" he jerked her toward him and spoke directly into her face. "N15m contract was lost because of you!"

"That is unfair of you. I tried to tell you your ego refused to…"

"Shut shut shut up. Just shut up!" he hit his head with his palm in a bid to control his anger. "Sometimes I hate you, you know. In fact, I I I …" he looked at her again and stomped right back out of the house.

"Temisan!" she called after him but he was gone.

What a waste? What a mess? What a … what a… She burst into tears. Why couldn't he just apologise first for a change.

What a loss! She sobbed.

Why don't you just apologise first? Women have more grace to apologise and to worship. It comes naturally for most of us. And if you don't have it, then marry a man who has, or develop the virtue. It is a virtue because it makes other virtues easy to display. Other virtues like submission and humility which are necessary to make the home sweet. One little word "SORRY" could have calmed a thousand storms. If he won't say it first, you say it. It won't reduce your spirituality or respect. On the contrary, it will increase it. And if anyone could humiliate you, better your husband than any one else. Headiness does not help any marriage. Whether it's from you or your husband but you can decide what kind of marriage you want. You can decide to stoop for your husband. Just remember that YOU STOOP TO CONQUER.

WISDOM FOR WOMEN

IF MY SON WAS MY STEP-SON!

MIMI SAT ON THE edge of her seat and poured the complaints like a flood. She was obviously frustrated by her dilemma with her husband's four year old son, Timi. As she narrated her tale, Tari was thinking about other things. She was lost in her thoughts by the time Mimi snapped,

"Aren't you listening to me?"

"I'm really sorry" Tari said in shame. She had in fact been listening but God was ministering something else to her. "Look, maybe you should just be more prayerful" she advised Mimi. She knew it was a bad piece of advice. She knew what she should tell Mimi but she felt a bit scared the latter would not be able to take the advice. It was just what the Holy Spirit had been ministering to her while Mimi talked.

"You seem so distracted. I will come back..."

Nengi rushed in and tripping over Mimi's feet fell into her mother's laps with the water colour in his hand. Tari had cursed before realizing what she said. Her new pink chiffon lace was splattered with a combination of colours. Nengi, her six year old son was notorious and restless. She felt like crying as she stared at her soiled gown.

"Oh Nengi!"

"Mummy, I'm sorry!" the boy exclaimed, picking himself up.

"How many times have I told you not to interrupt me when I have a guest?" Tari asked, frustrated. "Now see what you've done"

"I wanted to show you my…"

"How many times Nengi?"

"He's only a child" Mimi said forgivingly. "I'm sure the colour will wash off" she said looking at her friend's dress.

The softly spoken plea struck an odd note in Tari's brain.

If only Mimi would give her own step-son so much consideration, she wouldn't be complaining as she had been for over an hour to Tari. Mimi's step-son was not even half as wayward as Nengi!

If my son was my step-son, would I be able to:

☐ Understand why he should want to take double the snack I give my daughter to school because he loves food more than she does?

☐ Give him juice to school when my daughter prefers to take water?

☐ Have enough patience with his many irritating questions about things he obviously knew the answer to for instance, I am eating chocolate and he wants to beg for but first asks 'mummy, are you eating chocolate?'

☐ Forgive him when he, in his restlessness destroys precious things, like mistakenly tampering with an important cheque I'm about to cash in the bank?

☐ Free him if he beats my son up for provoking him so terribly?

☐ Still buy nice and expensive clothes for him though he is in the habit of getting them stained easily?

☐ Understand why he cries over unnecessary issues, gets moody and refuses food?

☐ Tell him I am sorry if I mistakenly hurt him physically or verbally?

☐ Sacrifice to buy him things (e.g. choir uniform) that other children have been asked to buy in order for them to participate in church programmes or playgroup occasions, outings, children's camp, books or other materials that other parents are buying for their children for a specific purpose?

⊡ To stand in as his mother if summoned to his school because of bad behaviour, especially if I have a choice not to go?

⊡ To scold him in love and not in anger when he misbehaves?

⊡ To give him direction and advice that will truly benefit him without any malice? Or rather look the other way and allow him to err so I will not be tagged a 'wicked step-mother'.

⊡ Eat from the same plate or in the same place with him on an outing, or finish first and then pass him the left over?

⊡ Treat him without preference to my son when I have to make a choice of who gets favoured before their father?

The list is endless but you find that many of us cannot do these simple things for our step-children. Do you have a step-child or children? I beg you answer these questions above and answer them sincerely. If most of your answer is NO, then you need to pray that God will help you love your step-child as your own. Most mothers have been able to do all of those points for their children. For the step-children, I speak as an advocate. God has placed them in your care for a purpose; don't disappoint God. Don't say, 'my son will never do this or that'. Instead, if you inherit a good and godly step-child, pray for him and encourage him, pamper him and make him feel free around you. If however he is an ungodly, wayward or stubborn step-child, rub off love on him, and then some. God who sees the heart will reward your long-suffering.

Remember, WHAT IF YOUR STEP-SON WAS YOUR SON?

WISDOM FOR WOMEN

CAN'T, WON'T OR SHOULDN'T FORGIVE!

IMABONG OPENED THE FRONT door of the house with high expectations. She wanted the carpenter to be through with their bad master bedroom door lock as fast as possible so she could have one or two more hours alone before the children came back from school. In her hurry, she didn't notice Eyo's 7-series BMW parked at an awkward bend behind their expansive duplex. They had condemned that part of the compound for parking because the driving space was so small. What would Eyo be doing at home at this time anyway? It wasn't part of the thought process. Talk about seeing with your mind.

"The first door to your left after the corridor. The lock got bad this morning. Go ahead, I'm coming" she told the carpenter who was also a member of their church. It was the man's first time in the private part of the house.

"Yes aunty" he said and followed the direction.

It was a very beautiful day in the often rainy city of Calabar. The sun was up early but not scorching. Cool west wind blew all through the beautiful, spacious house. It wasn't all that much a better delight being indoors, than being outdoors. Though an indigene of neighbouring Akwa Ibom State, Imabong had fallen in love with her husband's birth place the very first time she visited. They had moved their family of five to Calabar to take up a contract job at the massive TINAPA project; a dream business resort, the brain child of the incumbent state governor. Calabar was everything she dreamed of and more. The city was clean and green as they had often seen it advertised in Lagos. Serenity was one thing they had never really had, talking about the Lagos-factor. But not in Calabar. It was indeed a paradise city. Come And Live And Be At Rest; the acronym for CALABAR, indeed met up to its every word. They had been able to acquire a property almost immediately along ndidem usang iso road, a high brow area and 'Allen Avenue' of the paradise city. Though the beautiful estate had come at a heavy price, the worth of it was inconceivable. Imabong, who was an event planner, had opted to work from home, using the biggest of their three garages as her office. Though business had been slow, much slower than the hustle and bustle she was used to in Lagos, things had gradually picked up.

She dropped some files on the dining table and opened the refrigerator to pick a can of juice. She followed Mr. Akpan, the carpenter. When she entered the brief corridor, he was coming towards her, as though to leave.

"Did the door refuse to open?" Imabong asked. "You have to push a little. It's been stiff for days before it finally cracked this morn…" she stopped short and glared at the pale looking man.

"Aunty, I ur wah…"

"What's the matter?" she moved to the bedroom door and with more strength than was needed, pushed the door in.

The room was chilling… she hadn't left the A/C on when she was leaving.

Cold sweat covered her whole body at what she saw.

Eyo, scrambling suddenly, was stark naked with Ansa, their neighbour's eighteen year old daughter, in their matrimonial bed! Everything flew off Imabong's head. Her knees gave way and she slumped. She had never been so humiliated. Never been so cheated.

When she came to, it was Mr. Akpan who was fanning her. Tears streamed from Imabong's eyes. How could Eyo do this to her? In their home in their bed? She had told him she would go to Aba for shopping that morning but had decided to shift the trip to the next day due to an emergency job she had to quote for. It had skipped her mind to inform him of the change in plans. Even then, was this what he did whenever she was away, even for a few hours?

"Sir has gone. If you want to lie down I can help you to…"

"Mr. Akpan, thank you. You can go. I want to be alone. I can help myself. I'll be alright" she babbled.

"Are you sure ma?"

"Please, please leave…" she sighed heavily. Mr. Akpan headed for the door solemnly. He had never felt he was in a wrong place as much as this before. He was petrified. Eyo was an elder in the church. Imabong was women's fellowship secretary. He turned to look at her. She had buried her face in her palms and was sobbing bitterly.

Eyo returned to the house the usual time he normally did. He planned to pretend all that had happened in the day was a hallucination. A brutal joke by the devil on Imabong's imagination. He had his defence so well-planned, he was almost confident. As he stepped into his sitting room, he stopped in shock. The room was filled with guests; friends and family members. Imabong sat at one end of the heptagonal room. Their three daughters sat with his parents. Where did she get all these people from?! Suddenly, the spacious room became choking. Warmth and welcome which he had always felt in his beautifully and expensively furnished parlour became callous. Imabong went on her knees immediately and looked at each of the guests.

She said, "Please, my friends, my in-laws; give me one reason why I should forgive this monster"

Eyo knew the end was very near for his marriage. There could be no escape this time around.

Envisage, imagine, think sister.

Is it possible to forgive him for what he has done to you? For what he has done to your home, your relationships?

He is a pastor but he has made proposals and slept with half of the sisters in church. Is it possible to forgive?

No, he didn't sleep with half the sisters in church; he slept with his secretary, who's my friend. That's bad enough and is that forgive-able?

He slept with my little sister.

He slept with my mother!

I met him with two strange women in bed!

He's gay!!!

The question that arises in the place of forgiveness is not the magnitude of the sin but the individual ability to let it go. No matter whom the person involved is, the sin is as bad as it got. God frowns at sin. Sin is also sin. Adultery is as much sin as unforgiveness in the sight of God. This is why it is so painful when you hold back from forgiving the one whom you truly love. You hurt for the harm he'd done you, and then hurt from the guilt of un-forgiveness. It's good to know though that the ability to forgive is in-built. It is part of the God-nature in us. The Bible says that while we were still sinners, Christ died for us. At the same time, He also said He has given us the power to do even greater works than He did (John 14:12). While we are still pondering on this, Mt. 6:12 admonishes us to forgive those who hurt us as we seek God's forgiveness.

I can't forgive: This means you have tried but it seems so difficult or impossible to forgive. I believe that you trusted your man so much that what he did to hurt you completely stole your heart away. However, there is hope. The Bible says you should cast your cares upon Him for He cares for you (I Pet. 5:7). Ask Him to help you to forgive your man. It is possible and I believe you can do it.

I won't forgive: This is a conscious effort to withhold the act of forgiveness. It reveals the depth of the hurt and the attachment you have for your man. Each time you think about what he did to you, you stiffen and resist any form of weakness towards him. You refuse to pity or understand. You refuse to explore the possibility of releasing your man. I beseech you by the mercies of God, let go, and let God. God can handle anything and everything. Your prayers will be hindered, you will feel the pain all over again each time you try to push it away. Above all, you limit progress both for him and yourself. It's just not worth the stress.

I shouldn't forgive: This means you have successfully rationalized the whole situation and come to the conclusion that forgiving your man will not be worth it. You may think that not forgiving him will keep him bound and guilty, and so prevent him from falling into the same or similar mistake – this is not true. Tackling the problem this way, limits the extent to which you want God to help your man leave sin. After a while, he loses control and goes back to the sin. You may also think that he really doesn't need your forgiveness; after all, he misbehaves all the time. You may be right, but all the same, each time you forgive him, you draw him a step closer to pleasing God. It may be a journey of a thousand kilometres but it starts with a step forward in the right direction.

Frankly, whatever the sin or what you believe, it stands that rationalizing who or what to forgive is wrong. If God were to take count of sin, who will stand? We have all sinned and come short of the glory of God, yet while we were still in sin He forgave us. Don't try and take the laws of God into your hands. Pray that God will help you to forgive and move on.

My final word is that the spirit of unforgiveness is such a one that if you don't forgive, you can't move forward, the one you are holding in grudge cannot move on either. You cause a lot of traffic jam locating people for their blessing. You cause upset in the lives of these ones also.

Unforgiveness is just so much stress; it's not worth the stress either.

WISDOM FOR WOMEN

WHOSE WORD: HIS OR MINE!

KOMMA WAS SITTING IN front of her house, on the balcony, having her hair done by a hairdresser she was using for the first time. The weather had changed considerably from a cool, rainy wind to hot scorching sunshine and the two ladies sweated profusely. The hair style was 'shuku' with Ghana weaving and Komma hoped Owai would like it. In recent times, she had ceased to understand what he really wanted in her. Having been married for just three months, everything now seemed to be falling apart for them. Owai was almost always angry. Their relationship had started like a fairy tale; ending in their dream wedding, but the morning after had brought new realities to both of them. They no longer needed to court themselves. They were now together with a future they were both not sure of. Komma had not sensed the friction until it was almost late. She came from a family where there was love. Everyone watched over everyone. No one took their decisions alone. When serious decisions had to be taken, everyone had a say. But Komma never noticed Owai's deference to her style of life. While they planned their wedding, Komma made every step of the plans known to her family. They knew where they would spend their honeymoon, when and how. They knew virtually everything about the new life the couple would live. Prior to the wedding, Komma had lived and worked in Calabar as a lecturer but Owai lived and worked in Ikom as a bank manager. They had both agreed that Komma would move to Ikom and get another job. Until Komma's family stepped in and reasoned that it would be easier for Owai to move to Calabar and get a transfer from his bank, or better still, get another bank job.

"After all, Calabar swamps of banks" Komma's father reasoned. It sounded like a good idea to all of them. But when Komma suggested this to Owai, he clamped up, not refusing, not accepting. At the end of the day, both had kept their jobs and ended up living in different towns. Owai visited Calabar on alternate weekends. They had agreed that the weekends he did not visit, Komma would but Komma's father had cold feet about travelling…

"He's just being stubborn and proud. If he loves you, he should visit every week till he realizes how stupid that is and moves down"

So, Komma ended up seeing her husband twice a month.

Shortly after Komma finished her hair, her father came to visit. He loved the hair and praised it. Owai was due to visit the following week but Daddy had just finished eating when Owai walked in. It was a Friday and he usually came in on Saturday. And this was not his visiting weekend. But Komma was so glad to see him. She missed him dearly and would love to stay with him.

"You didn't call to say you were coming!" she exclaimed excitedly.

"Must I call before coming to my own house?" he retorted.

"Did something annoy you where you were coming from?" Daddy asked, concerned.

"No" he replied curtly. "Komma, you have to pack a few things. You are going to Ikom with me now"

"Now?!"

"That's what I said"

"Is there a problem?" Daddy asked.

"No problem, Daddy"

"But why the travelling now if there is no emergency?" Daddy pressed.

"I want my wife to follow me to Ikom now, is there a problem in that?" Owai faced Komma. She was shocked. He had never confronted her father so bluntly.

"Well, sit and relax. You'll eat something, won't you?" she made to leave the sitting room but he stopped her.

"I'll sit for as long as you're packing. I left work to come for you and I'm going back to work from here. Do you know you don't even know my house in Ikom?"

"But I visited before we got married?"

"But I told you I moved from there"

"Look Owai, why are you in such a hurry to take her to Ikom?"

"I'll tell you Daddy. We have a dinner tomorrow and my regional manager will be around and I want my wife to be there" Owai tried his patience.

"Is that all? But she has other things to do. Do you just barge in on her and make demands?" Daddy laughed.

"Daddy, please for once, stay out of this. Komma, I'm waiting"

"She's not following you, that's final. Don't you respect her feelings?" Daddy charged.

"Komma, I'll ask just once more, go and pack a few things. I'll bring you back after church on Sunday"

"Talking of Sunday, we have harvest and it is a special one. The Archbishop will be visiting and there will be communion…" Daddy started.

"Komma?"

"Daddy is right. I'm even singing in the choir…"

"Komma, what are you saying? Is it Daddy you listen to or me?" Owai shouted.

"What has come over you, Owai?"

"Listen to me carefully, if I leave here today without you, wife, you'll never see me again" he slumped into a chair. "I'll give you five minutes to pack"

Tears pooled in Komma's eyes and she looked at her father, confused. The older man nodded and she ran into the room to pack.

"I'm ashamed of you" he muttered to Owai but the latter had had it. He had come to Calabar with only one thing in mind, enough was enough. It was time for Komma to draw the line between the two most important men in her life. Either him or me, Owai thought.

Proverbs 14 verse 1 talks about a wise woman who builds her home and the foolish plucks it down with her own hands. You ask how I plucked down my home with my hands. One of the foolish ways to pluck down your home is by 'not' understanding whose word is law in your home. When you were single, your father had the last say but as a married woman, your husband is now your head. We should never make our husbands compete for our attention, especially with our family members. We are now one with him and any decision we take together supersedes any other person's. Some men have taken drastic decisions and 'banned' members of their wives' families from their homes. This should not be so. We women should be wise, not offending our parents but at the same time, making it clear to them that we are no longer under them. The marriage covenant favours two and not more than two. Princess Diana, in a TV interview once said her 'marriage was crowded' because there were three people in it. The covenant of marriage is for one added to one to remain one. You will be shocked to know that in marriage, one plus one plus one may be hundred and that indeed is a crowd. Whoever else has a say in your marriage can be a big threat to the success of that marriage; may be mother, father, family, friend, sponsor, whoever. It is left for us to draw the line. And to do it with caution and prudence. May the Lord help us; give us grace and wisdom in Jesus' name. Amen. Wisdom is profitable to direct!

WISDOM FOR WOMEN

HIS SECRETS ARE RUINING US!

SEGUN SWIVELLED DRAMATICALLY AND spoke in low tones as he usually did when he worked in his study. His bare feet rubbed against one another under the cheap hardwood table in the room and he blinked intermittently. All were bad signs. Bambo knew he could remain like that for hours; picking and making calls till he was ready to either go out or check in to sleep. Either way, she wasn't in his agenda. She entered the study with caution, feeling like Queen Esther entering King Ahasuerus' chamber without invitation. Today, she had prayed the prayer, if I perish, I perish. Segun looked at her warily, though he didn't break up the conversation. She stood uncertainly. Something told her to leave, before 'it is too late'. But she had to stay this time around. Something had to give, sometime.

Segun and Bambo had only been married for two years and they had a beautiful set of identical twin girls. Segun had said he was through with child bearing much to Bambo's chagrin. Her friend had told her he was joking, just wait and see. But she knew better. Her mother had offered to teach her how to 'plot coup' for him, she knew better too. The spiritual and all otherwise climate in their home was one and the same, Segun was boss, undisputed. Whenever she tried to seek advice on how to handle her husband, she always got into trouble with him. Sometimes, big trouble. He did not hit her yet, but she could weigh the emotional abuse he meted and beg to choose physical. Over the couple of years they had been together, Bambo had seen all sorts. He didn't cheat on her, no. but he deprived her of her joy, relaxation, and freedom to associate. Though he prided himself of being a very practical and understanding man, he had become more of a mirage to her. He had no friends at work or in church and hardly socialised with neighbours. It was always just them. He had politely requested that all members of her family stay away from them unless they were invited, and most recently, added a new feather to his cap. He made calls and took decisions without considering her.

"What is it?" Segun asked softly, looking at her. For an outsider, the blank look meant nothing. For Bambo, it was war! She wondered again, why she put up with his attitude. How she had missed it before they got married; or had she?

"We need to talk" she said. The room was cooling from the air conditioner but the heat that emanated from her body was good to fry.

"About?"

"Some auditors from your office came in today… to visit, they said"

"And?"

"Why would auditors come and visit you in the house during office hours?" she asked, disinclined. He had long stopped her from working at her bank job. 'Get a less stressful job or just trust me to take care of you' he told her. He did take care of her, though. She lacked… nothing!

"Did you ask them?" he swung to his feet in one fluid movement that made her jump. Segun towered above her. He was a hunk, with creamy chocolate complexion, well-built, muscled body, and an enchantingly handsome face. The very first time she saw him, she fell for him. Though huge, he had never used his physique to take advantage of her. If he had, he would have killed her. His hand alone was triple the size of hers.

"I couldn't have…"

"Look, Bam" he paused. He looked down at her. She wasn't petite for a woman with her 5'8 height and 70kg weight but with Segun, she felt more than look like an ant. "I am very busy right now. If there's anything you have to say…?" he shrugged.

"It's not normal, honey" she stammered. Why couldn't she come up with all the things she'd planned to say? Because he's standing right over you, and he can speak more than you and you are one highly intimidated woman! "I know you provide for me and the girls but I have been uncomfortable lately with the things you buy for us…" she said in one sweep. He continued to glare at her. She took advantage of the silence and spoke rapidly. "The other day, you took us out and spent almost fifteen thousand naira on just food and snacks…"

"You thanked me for it" he mumbled.

"I appreciate it but, honey, you can't afford it with your job…"

"You don't even know how much I earn so how can you know?"

"I don't know because you told me you could take care of us…"

"And I've been doing that"

She heaved. It was no use. He would turn round and round with the discussion and she would end up feeling stupid and not gaining anything. That's if he didn't lose his temper before then. When he lost his temper, he grounded the conversation and accused her of every mistake she ever made in their relationship, which were not few. She would end up apologising for days before they came back to the point where they could be cordial.

"Yes, you have and I really appreciate this. But, that refrigerator you brought home… I was in the market the other day and I entered a shop where it was on display… it cost over 600grand…"

"I bought it second hand from one of the big guns at work. I'm still paying for it…"

That burst her bubble. But there were other things. He recently moved them from their one-bedroom flat to a three-bedroom flat; he bought a bigger generator without selling off the old small one, he bought one additional air conditioner for his study, the treats have been more frequent; twice he made huge pledges in church and paid them up promptly, all in the past six months, and he made so many calls in hushed tones, daily.

"Look, honey, I'm not trying to imply anything or mistrust you but…"

"That's what it looks like!" he said and went back to his seat.

Oh no! "Honey…"

"I don't want to talk about this anymore I am beginning to get upset. Please, leave this room" he rubbed his forehead slowly.

"I'm sorry" she said and left the room. Back in the kitchen she burst into tears. God! His secrets will ruin us. I can feel it, God, help.

Two weeks later, Segun was arrested and locked up for a whole week. The auditors discovered he had been embezzling company funds. Most of the gadgets he bought in the house were confiscated. He lost the job after that.

Waoh! I am short of words now and I wish every man that comes across this will read. Men's secrets most of the time, get us ALL into trouble. I ask myself, but what can I do in this situation? I have prayed and fasted. If I report him, he may take… will definitely take offence in a big way that will end up causing more trouble than good. In addition, he will cook up good stories that will make me look like a fool! Huh uhn! My pastor will most likely compound the problem if he can't handle the problem…

First I'd like to say that our pastors should try more to help such families as this by making enquiries where they can into members who give beyond their means. He could be stealing to please God. But the end does not justify the means with God. God is holy and they that worship (with money and gifts) must do it in holiness.

Being married to a Segun is not easy and you need grace and mercy. I want to admonish us women to build confidence in ourselves. Men like this Segun start by destroying the confidence in their wives. They stop them from working, visiting, having friends, chasing the family away, and some even go as far as restricting their wives from church involvement and activities. A Segun I once knew even stopped his wife from coming to church while he was neck-deep in his department, faithfully serving God for both of them! Our confidence is in God and it will take a process to appreciate without being a threat to our man. The unfortunate thing is that such men also do not have much confidence. They are easily intimidated and base success on what they can or cannot do. We need to help them, by praying for them, submitting to them in the fear of God, correcting them in the spirit of love. Wives of such men have to be super women so that they will not be crushed and suppressed and end up suffering as much, if not more than the man because he will surely turn round and blame you for his misfortune! May God in His infinite mercy, help! Hebrews 4:16.

WISDOM FOR WOMEN

LEARN TO SAY THANKS!

I ALWAYS THOUGHT SAYING thank you was an easy thing to do. When we were growing up, my parents bought a game called "Happy Families" for us and made us play to help us cultivate the good manners of saying 'please' and 'thank you'. I do recommend that card game for every family. Anyway, I grew up knowing how to say thank you. Though I saw my education as my parents' responsibility, I told them, thank you. I also saw my upkeep as their responsibility, but I said thank you each time they gave me pocket money or bought things for me.

I didn't know it was difficult to say thank you until I got married. My husband is such a nice and considerate man that, before you make the request, he has already thought about it and most likely, done it! It was the attitude that brought me to great realization. I started expecting too much and when he didn't do a thing, I got upset.

We didn't have a house-help and I soaked the children's clothes overnight. When I woke up, my husband was having his quiet time. I took my time but when I realized he wasn't going to finish on time, I did my washing myself! Can you believe I was cross with him for not washing those clothes before I woke up! I took so many things for granted that when he did them for me, I forgot to say thank you. When he didn't, I took offence!

Consider this. You have your sister- or brother-in-law, living with you, and definitely, you expect a level of commitment from them when it comes to house work. Even if you have a paid help in the house, you expect your extended family to do 'something' around the house. You expect them to buy things and keep in the house if they are working, or at least, watch over something, anything around the house. The question is do you appreciate them if they do? My pastor once thanked me for counting him worthy to inform him about progress in my life, when I got engaged to be married!

He said, "As your pastor, you should inform me when you take such a big leap as this, but I want to thank you for doing the right thing!" Now I call that character! It is Godly!!

Sometimes we are tempted to feel it is not necessary to say thank you if the instructions are given by us or the initiative is from us. Especially if the person involved is a dependant or subordinate. Some of us find it hard to say thank you to our juniors. It really does not matter the age or status of this person, it is polite and godly to appreciate people.

Say thank you to your husband… it encourages him to do more.

Say thank you to your children… it encourages them to do more.

Say thank you to your extended family members… it encourages them to do more.

Say thank you to your in-law… it encourages them to do more.

Say thank you to those you are above… it encourages them to do more.

Say thank you to God… it encourages Him to do more.

Say thank you to those who are above you… it encourages them to do more.

Learn to say thank you.

WISDOM FOR WOMEN

WHEN HE STARTS REPORTING YOU!

"Whether you accept it or not, Ibo love marrying from Ibo. There's nothing you can say to convince me otherwise" Eneyi laughed.

"That is Ibo. I am Chidozie" he said softly.

Eneyi could never forget that day when she finally gave Chidozie her reply. It had been a 'No' and for good reason too. She had seen so many times inter-tribal marriages failing around her. Her aunt, Gina got married to a Delta-Ibo man and he married from his village three years into the marriage. Her uncle Ushie who married an Efik woman broke up with her barely six months into the marriage despite all the talk about the Calabar woman and her 'kopnomi'. Closer home, her best friend, Ohotu was struggling with her marriage to a Plateau man. Eneyi had been maid-of-honour in that wedding. No way, she had told Doz as he was fondly called but he would have none of it. Throughout the day, and all through the week, they argued.

Then softly in his compromising manner, he told her he would never give it up. And he never did. Eighteen months after that tussle, they were married in grand style. Eneyi never got to know how Doz convinced his family about her. In their village of Ogidi in Anambra state, you could count ten years and no inter-tribal marriage occurred. It was that bad! But Eneyi coped well. Life was good. Her parents-in-law were saints. When she delivered her first child, a boy, her mother-in-law spent three months. Three blissful months of which she could not believe her luck. When Mama packed to leave, Eneyi actually cried. If marriages were horses, Eneyi definitely was in for a long, sweet ride. All her friends envied her.

"If my husband was half as indulgent as Doz, I'll do thanksgiving in church" one said.

"I'm sending my Unimke over to Doz for extensive coaching" another told her.

"Inter-tribal marriages hardly work, yours is a research case" Aunt Gina chirped.

"However you do it, Eneyi, I envy you" Ohotu said, exasperated.

Ibo or no, Doz was the ideal husband. He made sure he provided for his family. His job as a sales man for a leading pharmaceutical company often took him out of town but Eneyi never had cause to worry. Doz was a responsible husband and father. He kept her informed of his every move. Sometimes when he had to travel at a minute's notice, he would drop by her office where she worked as a front office manager in a five-star hotel or call. It was thus a big surprise to Eneyi when, on a short notice trip by Doz, she received an anonymous call.

"Come and get your husband, I'm through with him" the lady said.

"Who is this?" Eneyi barked into the phone.

"Your arch rival. Please call your husband and ask him to leave my house" the lady said tartly and hung up. Eneyi was miffed. She called Doz and he picked it after the second ring. He told her he was out of town and in a pharmacy negotiating with his customers. He denied every allegation. The following day when he got back home, Eneyi threw tantrums about the issue. Doz calmly denied.

"I thought that was it. I believed him" she later told Ohotu.

BUT.

The phone calls continued. Sometimes, it would be late at night and the caller would request Doz' attention, and hang up before Eneyi could comment. It went on for a month and Eneyi found herself in a fix. Through the period, Doz denied the allegations.

One day, while at work, a family friend visited Eneyi at work. Pastor William was respected highly in the circles that associated with him, and the couple were no different. Eneyi excused herself from her office and followed him back to his.

"I would not have taken you out of your place of work if it wasn't important" he said. Eneyi knew there was trouble.

"It's okay. I hope all is well" she said.

"It shall be well" Pastor William sighed. "Your husband came to see me and it seems all is not well between you"

"What did he say?" Eneyi tried to be composed.

"Is all well between you?" Pastor William answered with a question of his own.

"To my own knowledge, I suppose" Eneyi stalled. What did Doz tell him?

"On his part, it seems all is not well" Pastor William launched. He had no plans to stall. "Your husband accused you of a lot of things, summary of which is that you are not a good wife" he said gently. Bells went off in Eneyi's head.

"He said that? When he's the one cheating?" she cried.

"Did you catch him?"

"He's been cheating because I have been receiving all sorts of calls from all sorts of people" she said.

"I don't know about that but I will confront him about it. But what went wrong? Why did he cheat? Was he always like that?"

"No, never. I am so surprised and scared stiff"

"He said you hardly sleep together" Pastor William looked away, embarrassed for her.

"What? My work for goodness' sake and his too. Is that why he went out?"

"I couldn't say he went out. He says you are stubborn, very stubborn because he decides to indulge you"

"Meaning?" Eneyi tried not to let off the steam on the pastor.

"That you do only the things you want"

"I have never done anything against his permission"

"He said he asked you not to take up this appointment, that he hates hotel work"

"Which job would I do then? Will I be sleeping and waking every-day…"

"He said he got you a good teaching job"

"I hate teaching" Eneyi spat out.

"You were good at it before you got the hotel job"

"Please Pastor William, you have not even heard my side of the story and you are already drawing conclusions"

"Do you cook for him?"

"He told you I don't because I have a lot of work to do in the house and a sister who helps thank God!"

"But he doesn't like her food" Pastor William trained his gaze on her. Trying to plead with her to understand his point.

"I have told him it's in his mind"

"You get away with it because he's simple, and I bet you, you don't want to lose him"

"So he told you he's been cheating right?" Eneyi's heart flogged the walls that confined it.

"I can't categorically say that but he wants you to try and change so your marriage can last"

"Is that a threat?"

"You may have to ask him, Eneyi. I don't really know"

A word is enough for the wise, they say. Marriage is like a garden owned by two people. You can't call it beautiful if a part of it is untended. That man you trust with your whole life may just one day begin to misbehave. The unfortunate thing here is you may not even see or hear anything until it's over! That's why when he starts reporting you, don't take offence.

He wants things to change. Many times, co-owners of the garden will fire the partner and employ another before the other party even knows they are out of business. When he gives you the privilege of reporting to someone he knows you respect, try and overlook his shortcomings and focus on yours, first. A man of God once said that marriages end when the man becomes unhappy. The truth is that we all want to be king in our own domain. Men especially are wired to rule, conquer, and dominate. If yours decides to judiciously mend his fence part of the garden, don't be the lacking party. Remember, God made you for him to be a helpmeet. To submit and to please… Huh! A good sign that he wants all to be well between you is when he vocalises it in the appropriate quarters. Do your part.

WISDOM FOR WOMEN

MANIPULATING MR. SIMPLETON

ZAINAB STOOD WITH ARMS akimbo and watched as Isaiah poured oil into the generator. A bead of sweat escaped his forehead and mixed with the thick liquid as it slicked out of the five-litre can.

"Are you sure we don't need a technician for this?" Zainab asked worriedly.

"It'll be alright. It had this problem last time…"

"And caught fire as soon as you switched it on" Zainab reiterated.

"It'll be alright" Isaiah repeated and straightened. "I hear your baby crying in the house. Maybe he's awake" he said, quietly dismissing her. She walked away with a hunch. He never listened, she thought warily. He was right though. Their six-month-old baby Gideon was wide-awake and groping in the darkness. She pressed a figure on her handset and used the illumination to light a candle.

"There, there" she cooed softly into the baby's hair as she opened her dress to breast-feed him. The lights came on even before she realised the generator was back on. "Oh thank God" she sighed as she straddled the tot.

Isaiah came back in with his shirt drenched in sweat.

"We need another generator" Zainab said, without acknowledging his effort.

"It's on my mind" he replied. He pulled the shirt over his head and took it to the laundry basket. "This room is a mess" he muttered. She took offence.

"You know how hard I try to keep this place neat. The room is too small. If I had more space I'll…"

"Don't bother" he breathed. He picked her clothes up from the floor and went about tidying the room quietly.

"Haruna came to the house when you were out. Hajia needs some money for her association's anniversary"

"Your mother should reduce the number of associations she's in" he sighed.

"If you'll only tell her"

"How much?"

"Three thousand naira"

"I'll get it for you tomorrow" the generator went out on its own. "Shit!" he cussed.

"I told you to get a technician" Zainab called after him as he left to check what the problem was.

"Fuel!" he called to her a few minutes later. "Thank God".

Zainab stretched out on the sofa in Jumai's house and hummed to herself. Her twin sister busied herself with the wool cardigan she was making for Gideon. The baby slept contented in the crook of her mother's arm, drops of breast milk hung on the corners of his full lips.

"Hajia said Isaiah gave her the 3k" Jumai said suddenly.

"With much ado" Zainab mumbled.

"What exactly is it with the two of them?"

"I don't know. He complains about everything concerning my family. Meanwhile his cousin Mustapha eats like a canker worm in the house"

"But you must give him kudos, at least. He tries. I mean, he has given Hajia almost fifty thousand naira for associations this year alone. I told her she had to cut down before she wearied your husband"

"Well, I know he will back off when he is wearied" Zainab replied sourly.

"That's not fair, you know. Isaiah gives everyone of us something regularly and only Mustapha benefits from him on his side of the family"

"Who's complaining Jumai? Mustapha's singular share equals the portion Isaiah gives all six children of my mother, so? His parents are dead. His brothers are multis. Who's complaining?" Zainab shrugged.

"I'm not" Jumai chuckled and the sisters shared the joke. "Just take it easy sha"

"Me? I don't have a problem o. When I need money, I pick his pocket, and he never knows" Zainab whispered.

"If he catches you!"

"He won't. Some days, I pick as much as 5k when he's in the bathroom, and he doesn't know" she laughed. "Oh, may God forgive me if it's a sin to steal from your husband"

"Why would you steal from him anyway? You are just plain greedy, that's all"

"He expects me to ask him for every dime. I want to buy water, I ask for twenty naira. I want to do my hair, I ask for two thousand. Huh!"

"He's a good man, though. He has a good heart"

"Huh, so says you" Zainab moaned.

"Don't take advantage of him" Jumai warned.

Some men just come as gifts wrapped in gold. They do all the odd stuff around the house, help with the children, help with the housework, provide for the comfort of the family and what have you. I call them Mr. Simpleton. Mr. Simpleton is your perfect example of a Christian husband and father. He's always there for you. Usually, a Mr. Simpleton is easy-going and gets so manipulated by his wife so much; you are almost deceived he enjoys it.

I've got news for you!

As good as Mr. Simpleton is, with several people envying his wife and children, he can snap at a moment's notice and often that will end his fraternity with 'goody goody'. Are you married to Mr. Simpleton? Do you feel nothing can shake your marriage? Are you totally trusting and leaning eternally on the joy that emanates from your home? Have you become slack and lazy at working on your marriage because of this? Watch out! I have met several Mr. Simpletons who cheat, deceive and tell lies to their wives. They go about it very quietly, easing off the pain of being married on their 'little' secret. When caught, they either whine and blame the wife, or break down and weep in repentance. More often than not, Mr. Simpleton's wife is usually his opposite and because of his character, she tends to take him, and a lot of things for granted because he would scarcely reprimand her. Indulgence is usually a norm around the house but when Mr. Simpleton decides to fight back, he breaks every code of discretion. A Mr. Simpleton I once met, after his wife confessed that she 'defrauded' him in bed, was caught several times with other 'sisters' in church to the ignorance of the wife. He messed around so wildly, he became known for it!

This article is dedicated to every woman married to a Mr. Simpleton. As easy as it is to stay with them equates the ease with which they can ruin us, if they are pushed to the wall. Mr. Simpleton wants the level of dedication he gives to the marriage. Don't test him just because he conforms all the time. When he decides to strike back, the damage may be worse than those who hurt their wives more regularly. After all, we do know that pretenders tend to exaggerate the situation.

WISDOM for SINGLES

Pr 8:11 For wisdom is better than rubies, And all the things one may desire cannot be compared with her.

Dedicated to my Sister-in-law:
Moji Aizobu
A lady of style

Cover Concept by Amazingrafiks © 2009

CONTENTS

WISDOM FOR SINGLES

MOVE ON!

Sisi carried Mimi on her laps and smiled softly. The pastors looked first at her, and then at the tot on her laps. She knew what was going on in their minds. Who owns this? She decided to meet their gazes one after the other, five of them altogether; with an easy smile though inside her stomach were tiny knots of nerve that seemed to be there to stay. A lady she had seen minister in church several times, one of the pastors, blurted out unethically.

"Whose child is this? Thought you said you were single"

"I am single but this is the second of my twin-children. I had them two years ago to a man I thought I would marry. He was on youth service. He left with a promise to return but I haven't seen him since. I have decided to move on with my life" Sisi gave the speech with great confidence, assessing the reactions of the pastors as she went along. This was auditioning for the choir and she needed them to know she could compose herself properly. In her, they saw self-esteem as clear as day. She had seen this sort of response to honesty before, especially amongst fellow Christians. People appreciated honesty. But she hadn't always been able to be honest about her dilemma all along.

She had met Efosa when he first strolled into her father's estate agency almost three years earlier, clad in the NYSC attire. He was a tall man, almost 6'5 and with broad and heavily built muscles. He had a healthy face with lots of hair; side burns, moustache and beard. The dark-complexioned face looked crowded but mightily handsome. She remembered she stood by her father's secretary's desk that day, waiting to receive a letter of appreciation she would give to her father for his generous donation to her school club; when he walked in. They both looked up and at him and instead of a greeting, he rubbed his face self-consciously and chuckled,

"I need a shave badly, I know"

The two ladies had burst into laughter, indulging him; from that day, they had become friends and then, intimate.

Efosa, though a native of Edo state had grown up in Lagos and favoured himself to be a Yoruba boy as he spoke the language fluently. As soon as he got her name, he started calling her 'Sisi Eko', and they grew very fond of one another. He got the job as an estate agent putting his full discipline in law into practice. Before then, he had never been to Portharcourt and Sisi derived pleasure showing him around. He was her dream come true and expressed love for her the way she had never seen. First to her was the gross respect he had for her. He never made demands on her. All her previous boyfriends had asked to sleep with her but not Efosa. He treated her with caution and accepted her for all she was worth. And to him, she was worth a lot. Their relationship bloomed from there. They went everywhere together, and people knew them as a couple. Sisi, a final year student of accountancy started looking forward to a life with Efosa. Her parents loved him for his charms and his focus.

When it came close to the end of Efosa's service year, Sisi started feeling she wanted more. Since he came, he had not visited home and had told her he wanted to get back from service before he talked about her to his family. Hers had accepted him head to foot. As so it was that Sisi, in a moment of emotional need, gave her body to Efosa. It was her first time, and he was so grateful to her for counting him worthy.

"I will always love you" he murmured inviolably.

For the remaining month of his stay in Portharcourt, they were sexually active. When Efosa got back to Lagos, he called her regularly, promising his love and devotion and asking her to give him time. Initially, he used his job search as an excuse. Then he got a job with a foreign graphics design firm as a legal assistant. It then got down to convincing his parents he was ready for a wife. And three months passed. It was then she discovered she was pregnant. Scan results showed that it would be a multiple birth. She was excited and told him it was the perfect reason for her to visit his family. That was the last time Sisi ever heard from him. Though he had sounded just as excited, each time she called after that, his phone was unavailable. She started feeling uncomfortable. She called him from different networks until her friend told her he'd probably thrown the line away. She decided to take the bull by the horn and travelled to Lagos. She had an address, for his office and home. She went straight to the office. She was told he was not around. When she traced his home, she met his mother who told her simply that they had never heard of her and Efosa never mentioned a relationship to them. The mother was outrightly rude, short of shooing her off their property. She stayed with a friend and for a whole week, visited Efosa's office. Each time, she waited for hours to see him after being told he was either busy or out of the office. At the end of the week, she returned to Portharcourt, broken-hearted. Her parents stood by her in every way and that was where she drew strength.

"I have moved on" she fixed her gaze on the female pastor on the panel. "I have never heard from him but I sent a letter to his office and one to his home telling him about the twins. I never got a reply. My mother took care of my children while I went for youth service and now I'm here, sitting for this interview" she turned her gaze to the senior pastor. "I have come a long way since then. I have established for myself a durable business that I enjoy, working for myself. I am happy and it will only get better" she smiled. The pastor nodded in approval.

Sisi got a placement in the choir.

If you start waiting for every disappointment to wear out before you do, the greater chance is that you'll wear out first. Move on! It's one of the hardest things to do in life but you've got to. You are fearfully made, and if no one appreciates you now, the right person soon will; which is the most important anyway. God has set you up for great things ahead and you can't afford to allow any man or woman to shift your focus. Discover God's purpose for your life. Fit yourself into it, and move. Move on!

FACE IT, BROTHER; SHE DOESN'T WANT YOU!

Osaz was so excited about his upcoming wedding. Omasan was such a beautiful woman: soft-spoken, petite, polite, and a great cook. Even though he had not tasted her food before, he had heard enough to convince him of her prowess with raw food.

He told people around and expected everyone to be glad with him. He had fixed the wedding date and even chosen his best man. The only pending problem – which he knew would be solved quickly – was Omasan's consent. They had been friends earlier but as soon as he mentioned marriage, she withdrew. His friends tried to discourage him after this.

"She's snobbish" some said.

"She's strange" others told him.

"You two are not compatible" his pastor admonished. But he loved her. He was crazy about her, which seemed the most important to him. He knew he would win her with time. Even though she had turned him down three consecutive times, he understood the psychology of women. They loved to be hounded! He decided to go on with his wedding plans. Omasan would fall into God's purpose for their lives with time...

Sadly, the wedding day Osaz fixed came and went. Omasan is married to someone else today.

The above story sounds like fiction but it's not. Unbelievable! I hear someone saying Osaz is MAD. Well, to some extent, you might say that, but he is actually suffering from an advanced stage of infatuation. He has dreamt so much about Omasan that it is now 'turning his head'. It is a rare case because when a man is infatuated, he takes it more as a challenge, and so he pursues it. And this is why the disease is usually hard to detect in men. They follow it up just to satisfy their ego. They refuse to admit it is mere infatuation.

Sometimes women add to the complication of this 'lust' in men by indulging them. If you know a man is fascinated with you, and the feeling is not mutual, it is wrong for you to take gifts from him. Ho ha! Instead, you take car rides, follow him to Biggs, and Happy Bites, Royal Chinese, enjoy treats, follow him to meet his parents, and dilly-dally around him! Haba, this is unfair.

Every relationship stands a test of time, if it is ordained by God. My advice is to play on time. Infatuation is like fish out of water when tested with time. It dies off quicker than you think. Watch the lady. Does she seem excited around you? Is she as taken with you as you wish? Does she pay attention when you are talking? Does she seek your opinion about matters that concern her life, and general issues? Or, she is particularly interested in helping you spend your money… and nothing more? Be sincere.

But, be careful! Don't over flog the test as you may lose her.

Watch and Pray!

FACE IT, SISTER; HE DOESN'T WANT YOU!

TARI SAT UPRIGHT AND pasted a smile on her wide lips. Her two dimples went on display immediately. Her heartbeat increased by half as the team leader, Timi entered the office. No, actually, he only peeped in. Perhaps to check on who was in and who was not. His gorgeous male cologne wafted to her nostrils and she almost closed her eyes in ecstasy. Good God, she thought, everything about him was fantastic.

"Hi" his deep masculine voice carried to where she was and she bit her lip. Before she could find the words to reply, he snapped the door shut. The click made her jump in her seat, and she discovered she was sweating in her palms. What was wrong with her? She was always nervous around Timi. Jumpy. Stupid. Tongue-tied. Nervous. She sighed wearily; he must think she's a jerk.

Timi had always been nice to her, and probably every one on the team. He was hardworking, committed and a pace-setter. Ever since she got the job as an architectural assistant in a big building conglomerate, she had been enthralled by his swift and focused devotion to targeted goals. But it wasn't until the day she needed his assistance on a shopping mall project she was handling and he'd stepped in, saving her from embarrassment in front of the whole team. Her presentation had been mistakenly miscalculated and Timi had worked all night in the office with her to make sure the clients got the right archetypal of the building when they came in the following morning. She had bought him a 'thank you' card and expecting nothing of it, was thrilled at the way he made a 'big do' about it. But she soon realized that was the person of Timi. When Esther, the accounts assistant ran into problem with the auditors, Timi mediated, even though he was on the accounts team. But this did not diminish her admiration. If anything, it grew, and grew and grew. And she noticed he began to withdraw from her. The more she tried to get him close, the more he became cold towards her!

Infatuation, as against our better judgment, is not a teenage problem alone. Many professionals get infatuated easily. This age long disease has been with us and the earlier we accept the cure for it the better. For some of us, we contacted it early enough and got delivered sooner than it had the chance to damage us. Truth is we all contact this disease at some point in our lives. Some as early as in primary school, some as late as after marriage! Some once and for all, some intermittently. The sad truth is that some get infected when they really need a husband. Now that is hard.

Let's face some facts about infatuation:

▢ Infatuation is a mirage. It is not real. It does not last.

▢ The person feeling it will be 'burning' while the 'prey' may or may not notice. The better for you if he doesn't.

▢ If not handled quickly and properly it may lead to mental psychological illness, physical illness, emotional imbalance, embarrassment, and shame, or public disgrace.

You see, there are many sisters like Tari out there, feeling sorry for themselves that their Timis' don't want them. Or perhaps he hasn't noticed them, and 'fallen' for them as they have. Truth is it may not even be his fault. He may not have seen you at all. Maybe he just sees you as any other pretty sister on the team, in the office, in the church, in the fellowship, in the ministerial council, wherever, whatever. No strings attached!

Sister, I want to help you.

Face the fact: he doesn't want you. If he does, he will come after you. It is not your 'behaving funny' around him that will make him notice you. Even if he does at that, there may be no appeal. Take time to develop confidence in yourself. If he wants you, he will come after you.

Better deny yourself of thinking about him than allow the unreciprocated feeling torture you.

WISDOM FOR SINGLES

ANOTHER MAN'S WIFE

VICTOR LOOKED THROUGH THE window of the house on Third Avenue and sighed heavily. She should come on time, he thought wearily. What would he do if she didn't? This was meant to be the last time. This time, they would call it off. She'd said so and he had resigned his mind. Of course he loved her but he couldn't pray for her husband to die, neither could she get a divorce. And the guilt she was feeling was beginning to affect their relationship. The last time they mated, she had burst into tears. The previous time before then, she'd been so quiet; he had felt as much of the guilt. He'd told her then they could not continue if she would keep thinking about her marriage. She had promised not to the next time. But something had happened at home and when they finished making love, she had burst into tears, inconsolable. They had both agreed it had to be over.

Antonia had been his old girlfriend in school and after he finished, he'd travelled out of the country. He had not intended to break up the relationship but the pressures abroad weighed him down and he lost touch with her. When he came back after a few years and attempted to find her, he discovered she was married. He wasn't sure if it was love or just the male ego that pushed him to chase her all over again. And like the first time, he won her heart. They were secretive about the relationship. They had to be, and despite the fact that they were now both believers, their fleshly lusts prevailed. Antonia and her husband, Rufus attended different churches and this fuelled her availability to Victor. Whenever Rufus went for evening service, Antonia headed for the house on Third Avenue, a secluded apartment belonging to Victor's senior brother who was resident with his family in the States. Victor as caretaker of the apartment had refused to rent it out as his brother had issued, giving flimsy excuses. Instead, he used it as a hideout love-nest. Whenever there was also evening service in Antonia's church, she met with Victor. They had tried to break up several times without luck and decided to allow things to work out themselves but with the weight of guilt on Antonia, they could wait no longer. Victor had requested one more meeting. The last one. To love her one last time...

He checked his wristwatch again. She was an hour late already. Maybe she wasn't coming. Maybe her husband didn't go to church today. Maybe she just couldn't bear to see him again. They'd been on for six months. Six months! And to him, it seemed like yesterday. She wasn't happy. No one would blame her. He had only thought to make her happy. He slouched onto the sofa in the room and waited, his heart thumping. A bad feeling told him she was in deep trouble. No, they were very careful. She couldn't have run into trouble. He shook his head. No.

Two hours later, Antonia called from her hospital bed. Rufus had followed her to the house on Third Avenue and just as she pulled the gate open, closed in on her. After getting a confession out of her, he battered her ruthlessly on the road. The street was deserted and no one had heard her muffled cries. It was finally over she told him. Luckily, Rufus had not wanted to know who he was. She didn't have any broken bones but it sure felt as though she had, and her face was blown up like full-term pregnancy.

What hurt Victor most as he clung to the handset and wept long after she had hung up was that he had been so close to helping her out of her husband's fury or at least sharing the pain.

Jealousy is the rage of any man. Imagine if it was your wife someone else was 'using'. Forgive the raw term but it is painful. And it happens everyday and everywhere. Single ladies are 'sleeping' with other people's husbands and single men are 'sleeping' with other men's wives. Stop and think and imagine, were you to be the victim. How would you feel? It is unfair, least to say it is ungodly. As soon as you marry, you become the jealous, possessive spouse, trailing your partner all over town and sniffing around because you know. You know you are GUILTY! Your bad behaviour is wrecking lives and homes. You are against God's plan and purpose for marriage. You are God's enemy! It does not matter why you do it or did it. Financial support is not an excuse. Emotional need for love or protection is not an excuse either. No excuse is good enough for stealing what belongs to another man or woman. You need to repent. Be sorry. Turn from your evil ways and let God cleanse you. The prayer here is to uproot the evil you have sown and to burn all old bridges. Seeds grow and bear fruits and the devil remembers! And if you are doing it, STOP.

PLEASE.

WISDOM FOR SINGLES

THAT ELEMENT OF FEAR

THE FIRST TIME TEDROS addressed Ayana in the presence of Azmera, she cringed literally shrinking. They had been out at the mall, shopping and Tedros had asked Ayana for his sister's shopping list. Ayana had stammered a flimsy reply.

"What?" Tedros asked his voice hard.

Ayana fumbled in her bag, knowing the list was not there.

"I remember the things she…"

"Where in God's name is the list?" Tedros snapped.

"I was sure I picked it on the table" she murmured, looking at him. Azmera could not believe the look on her face. It was short of describing ethereal.

"For Chrissakes!" Tedros yelled, causing one or two shoppers to stare.

"You're causing a scene, Ted. I'm sure I can recall" she said urgently.

"You know my problem with you" he lowered his voice but it was still as potent. And when he took a step closer she held her breath with a wheeze, like someone who feared being hit.

"You never accept" he said into her face.

"Please Tedros, you are making me uncomfortable. If you don't mind" Azmera stepped behind Ayana and sighed. "If you can remember, then let's pick up"

"Shouldn't we really" Tedros said with spite and walked away angrily. Azmera was shocked. "Was he upset about something?"

"No" Ayana shrugged. "I shouldn't have forgotten the list" she sighed.

"I can't believe this. For goodness' sake, we can call his sister and get a dictation. Are you sure it's nothing more than the list?"

"Come on, he'll be wondering what we are still doing" Ayana said and followed her fiancé.

What piqued Azmera was more the fact that the two were not even married yet. She kept the belief to herself that Tedros must have been in a bad mood that day. The opinion was just beginning to stick when Ayana called Azmera from the University of Nairobi campus where they both studied Law. Azmera had gone to visit her parents and was relaxing when the call came in.

"Please can you come over to school? Please it's urgent" Ayana said, close to tears. There was noise in the background.

"Come for what? You know I just got here" Azmera sighed. She couldn't understand her friend.

"I forgot to tell you that Ted would need the car this afternoon…"

"No, Ay. You told me I could borrow your car for the rest of the day"

"That's what I'm saying, I'm sorry" Ayana whispered.

"This is just not fair" she dragged her feet up. "I just got here and now I have to travel hundred kilometres all the way back just for nothing" as she said it, her anger towards her friend rose. "I mean, if you'd told me this, I would have come on my own instead of…"

"Please now. Understand"

Azmera heard the tears and hated herself for getting angry. Even more she hated Ayana's vulnerability. What on earth is so special about the Tedros anyway? Why couldn't Ayana leave the guy alone? She had always noticed that carefree attitude in the way Tedros treated Ayana but this was beginning to suck! As she got angrily into the car, shouting a quick explanation to her mother, she decided to sit Ayana down, and talk real sense into her.

There is what I call 'that element of fear' necessary in every relationship. When it's not there, problem is inevitable. For numerous reasons, people get into the relationship they get into. Some for wealth, fame, status syndrome, desperation, ignorance et.c. the list is inexhaustible. However, when you are in a relationship that is serious and heading towards marriage, there are some tips to look out for which are important ingredients for keeping the relationship stable. The element of fear is one of them. Fear here is that feeling of trepidation that comes out of love and respect. Because you 'fear' a person, you don't want to hurt the person. You don't want to upset the person; you don't want to be in the person's 'bad books'. So, you do things that will guarantee the person's joy. It's just a small element of it that's needed. And how do you know if there is an element of fear in your relationship, both sides inclusive? You study the way this person treats you in public. How does he talk to you in the presence of others? How considerate is she of your schedules and budget? And some other little things like the choice and tone of voice they use to address you; in public and in private, how they regard your friends and family members…

Bottom line is, don't settle for less. If you don't like the way they treat you, either deal with it, get out of the relationship, or resign yourself to whatever you get and don't blame anybody but yourself!

TORN BETWIXT

Selina's thoughts were far away, farther than any of her friends or family members could imagine. Her confusion went beyond the physical, she afraid, they were becoming spiritual. And that was quite scary. She had never prided herself as being sophisticated. Despite the fact that she came from a ruling family in her hometown and a prestigious one too, she was just simple. And her love for Obase had been as simple as that. When they had met at a family occasion and had gotten introduced, it had been an instant hit, one that pleased both families. Obase's father had been as much involved in politics as Selina's was in royalty. The two families had done great things for the small town of Okwuosi, bringing connecting roads to neighbouring cities, electricity, and portable water. At the state level, Selina's father sat with the governor and members of the state executive council. Very few other chieftains had the privilege.

Selina's love life till now had been uneventful. As a final year student in the high school, she had dated a boy in her class for as long as they waited to get admission into university, after that, they had parted ways. She got admission into the Nigerian Defence Academy; he went to University of Uyo. They lost touch after that, and that was it. While at the Academy, she gave her life to Christ, and her romantic expeditions took a significant downward turn. Selina, though an African beauty of unique facial and physical qualities, something, maybe her quiet attitude, somewhat kept the men at arm's length. Being in the army did not help her either, not as though it bothered her. Obase, who was coincidentally a civilian medical doctor with the army in another location, had quite a lot to talk to Selina about. Their match was short of one made in heaven by none.

But after three years of courting and not quite getting round to the wedding ceremony, everyone was getting weary, including Selina. Initially, she wanted to get to know Obase better, then she went for an eighteen-month training abroad and then started settling down and waiting on her application to get transferred closer to Obase.

On the fateful day when she walked into defence headquarters on summons, only one thing caught her attention. The army captain that stood leisurely, chatting with her commandant's secretary. He was tall, dark, and handsome, straight out of a fantasy novel. His voice was low and deep and his laughter, when he did, rumbled through the room. She had filled the form and sat quietly, waiting to be called. She had not been told what she was wanted for but it was usually one of a couple of things; her transfer had been approved, or it hadn't been and they wanted her to know why or resume on another…

"Hello" he had stooped very close to her face and smiled "my name is Ron, you?" he asked softly, and had stolen her heart from there. They had exchanged phone details and talked almost every day for two weeks.

Her problems were many. She had never taken a liking to any person at first sight, without even talking to the person. She hardly missed anyone, not even Obase. She had never spent so much time on the phone with anyone before. Ron had scored several firsts with her. He was kind, and decent. He was handsome to a fault… no, wickedly. He was military, though an account officer and not combatant like she was. He was Christian. Most importantly, her heart flipped like never before.

But he was trouble!

She had put in almost three years into her relationship with Obase, and besides Ron, he was like stale bread. In the two weeks of talking with Ron, she could hardly have a decent conversation with Obase. She felt guilty. Even though she had gotten her transfer, she had instantly felt a deep remorse about it.

One mind told her Obase was good for her. He was civilian, dependable and they had been committed to one another for long. The other mind told her to stop being cliché. She now knew what love was like. She was excited to her bones about Ron. One voice accused Ron of being a home breaker; the other praised him for discovering who she really was. She was distracted, and could hardly pray. Though she had resumed and reported at the barracks where Obase worked, she didn't derive any joy in it. All she wanted was to go back to her former base, to be closer to Ron.

She knew everyone would be shocked and think she was mad if she did exactly what she was itching to do.

Resign from the army.

You know, it is not about who he is or what he has, or what he can do. It's all about you. Who are you? What do you have? What can you do? There are many strange bed-fellows in marriages of today; people who have been constrained to do what the society expects, what the church expects, what the pastor expects, what their friends expect, what their families expect!

What do you want?

Marriage is an institution of choice. Don't allow anyone to draw you in or else it becomes quick sand. And you'll be shocked how fast it can overwhelm you. Make your choice based on what you want because you are going to be held responsible. When the Bible says the two shall be one, it means it. No matter how close a third person is in your marriage, the fella can't be one with you and your wife, or you and your husband. Don't take this issue lightly. Prayerfully make the right choice.

You need to.

WISDOM FOR SINGLES

LIVING IN A TEMPTER'S WORLD

AKOSUA SAT AT THE table in the fast food restaurant and punched furiously on the keys of her handset. Was she dreaming? Five hundred rand gone so fast? What did she buy? How was she going to cope for the next few weeks? Quickly, she converted the amount to cedis mentally and rolled her lovely, big eyes. Mama would never be able to raise that anytime soon. How was she going to survive? She uncrossed her long legs once and then crossed them back. Suddenly, sweat broke out on her forehead. She opened her bag and brought out a perfumed handkerchief. Murmuring to herself, she dabbed her forehead quickly and placed the kerchief back in her bag. One of the uniformed waiters, the enthusiastic one who had excitedly chased her to a seat when she first arrived almost half an hour earlier, approached her table slowly and looked at her knowingly.

"Do you want to place your order now?" he tried to smile.

"No" she said sharply. "I mean, sorry. Not yet. Please" she wasn't even sure she had enough to pay for food. Unless her phone calculator was faulty. She had giddily pushed behind her the nudging voice that told her to slow the shopping down. And she would never be able to tell Mama to... What? Her mother worked hard to keep the family together, despite the fact that they were in a foreign country and many people at home believed they were millionaires in South Africa. Well, in cedis, they were but not here. After Papa lost his job to a careless mistake, Mama had catered for all four of the children, paying bills, fees and coping with Papa's indifference and anger. Sure it brought strains to the marriage and the home but no one was complaining loud.

"Not even a drink?" the young waiter politely pressed.

"Please. I need to be alone for a while" she snapped. It wasn't the boy's fault. What she just spent in two weeks was meant for a month and other concerns, clothing, personal effects and so on.

"It's just that…" he started.

"You want to send me out?" she asked, annoyed.

"No way, Miss" the boy said quickly. "When you're ready" he backed away.

"You could order the drink now anyway" a voice said above her. Her head jerked up to tell the person off, thinking it was another waiter or a supervisor. Instead she came face to face with Olaitan.

"Excuse me?" she glared at him. He was a tall, dark-skinned, middle-aged man, dressed in what looked like very expensive white shirt and tan trousers. The jacket he wore over the shirt was brown leather. His presence was imposing, his frame, attractive. Very attractive.

He flashed a smile. "May I?" he stated politely and took the seat opposite her.

"Do I know you?"

"My name is Olaitan Damien. I am a medical doctor from Nigeria, though I've live in South for eight years now" he said.

"I see. And how may I help you?" she asked sarcastically.

"I was going to make you order a drink, to start"

"Make me?" she snickered at him but there was no arrogance in his tone or attitude. In fact, his smile was warm and engaging, exposing strong, white, even teeth.

"I've been watching you since you walked in. You are a very beautiful lady" he said softly. No way, she thought. He looked old enough to be her father and she spotted the wedding band on his left hand. No. Go.

"I have to go. Nice meeting you" she stood up.

"Wait, please" he looked up at her. Nothing else could have stopped her except the pleading in his eyes. She sat back down. He waved to her waiter and he shuffled over, taking her food and drink order.

Over the meal, he made small talk with her. She wanted to preach to him but he said he already knew the Lord. In fact, he mentioned the name of his church and she was impressed. It was one of the biggest churches in the country with branches all over the world. Well, well, God has sent an angel. His family shuttled between Nigeria and South Africa. His wife was a business woman and like she had thought, he had a daughter close to her age.

When the waiter came with the bill, he brought out a wad of bills; she had never seen anyone bring out such an amount in rand. He paid the waiter and left an exorbitant tip. Then he offered to take her home.

And told her he was in love with her already. And was willing to do anything for her.

An answer to all her financial needs and troubles? Or a tempter in his full prime.

Temptation is… just that. Temptation! You can't excuse it; you can't rationalize it; you can't overlook it! It's dangerous, treacherous and please don't play with it. When I was growing up, novels, and lots of societal opinion led me to believe that only women seduce. What a rude awakening it was for me when as a young woman, I came head-on, colliding with men who are perfected in the art of seduction. It takes your every iota of will-power to resist, better still, run! He is a smooth-talking brother. He has all the right answers to all your burdensome questions. Contrary to all the single brothers around you, he knows how to treat a lady. He speaks in tongues like tongues of fire and does his quiet time every single day. Listen to me; he is your perfect example of a tempter. You have nothing to do with him! He belongs to another woman.

LEAVE!

WISDOM FOR SINGLES

A CLASSIC LOVE STORY

It was your usual day; sunny and hot like hell was coming down to take over earth. In the midst of the hustle and bustle of the market, Tsema was hurrying to finish up her shopping to catch up with end of lunch time. She was sweating like a Christmas goat and what else. She dodged sweaty bodies like hers to no avail. She was rough and scratchy and wondering what her boss would do if she entered the office looking as dirty as she now felt. Or was it just an over-reaction of her pulses? She was sure her perfume was worn out, what with rubbing bodies with regular market people. She wondered why there were so many people in the market at this time of the day. Did people not go to work?

"Goodness gracious!" the deep voice groaned with suppressed fury. She turned in time to face the hard, sweaty face. The man held his shirt front away from his body and Tsema also groaned in disgust. Smashed eggs drooped all the way down from the man's starched white shirt to the ground.

"Did I do that?" Tsema asked as people dodged the mess on both sides of the narrow market aisle, forcing her to stand closer to the imposing bundle of anger in front of her.

"What did you think?" he bit out. She got angry then. Even if she wasn't exactly looking where he was going, wasn't he? He was just as much to blame as she was!

"Well, let's get you out of here before more irritating accidents happen" she snapped and headed off in the direction of the exit. She would buy two packs of pure water and spray her perfume on him; that should take him home.

She hurried through the crowd and when she got to her car in the parking lot, she was desperate. She turned round and bumped right into him. He was fuming.

"Can you not apologise, arrogant lady?" he said stiffly. "I have a board meeting in fifteen minutes, how do you reckon I get to it smelling like damn chicken eggs?"

"How indeed?" Tsema replied with as much heat. "If you were looking where you were going, you won't be in this trouble. Besides, doesn't a man like you have a little, submissive wife in the house who'll do all your silly shopping, cooking and cleaning?" Now why did she say that? She thought warily as soon as the words left her mouth. She looked up at his face and he was just as shocked as she was at the nasty question. They had never met before…

"I'm sorry I said that" she shook her head sadly. "I'm just tired and angry at myself. I'm sorry for bumping into you, smashing your eggs and…"

"I wasn't looking where I was going either" he interrupted her. He sounded so sorry she looked up at him again and burst into laughter. And he joined her. "I'm sorry for calling you arrogant. My name is Tokunbo Igba"

"Tsema Okoli" she said. "Say what, my house is just round the corner from the market. I could get you one of my brother's shirts to wear for that meeting of yours" she offered.

"Really, that would be great. I'm actually facing a bid panel and I know I'll lose that bid if I show up like this"

"Let's go then, do you have a car or we go together?"

"I'll follow you in my car"

"Ok" she started to enter her car.

"That little wife you talked about" he stood and stared at her. "I think it's a great idea". He turned and rushed to his car. She stared after him before she realised she was staring and smiled.

Tokunbo won the bid and invited Tsema for a celebration dinner in his house. When she arrived, she discovered she was the only guest.

"So, where's everybody?" she asked as she received the cold drink he put in her hand with a smile.

"Everybody?" he feigned ignorance. "Did I tell you there would be other people?"

"No way. You said it was a celebration party…"

"Party for two"

"You are a conman. When you say party, I expect at least thirty people" she laughed.

"Ok ok, I give up. It's a party alright. Guests will arrive in an hour. I wanted us to have this time alone… you know, get to know one another better. I've looked for every reason to have this alone time with you, but, well, it's been a month since the market thing, you know" he stammered.

"I know" she smiled.

"Oh, don't give me that look. I don't get jittery around women, usually" he walked away from her and put space between them.

"Usually" she said patriotically.

"You want me to make you uncomfortable? Don't try me at this game"

"Not at this game, no"

"Tsema" he breathed deeply and laughed. "I feel so nervous. I've not thought about anyone but you, since"

"Well, what set you thinking so much about me? Is it because of the eggs you lost?" she joked.

"I want us to be together. I feel such a connection with you" he said softly.

"I don't even know you" she shook her head. "Let's just start off being friends and…"

"I don't believe in all that being friends and all" he moved closer to her but still stood awkwardly at a distance. "I know you love God. I believe you are born again" he wasn't asking. "I see a passion for God through your eyes. If I ask you to marry me, I don't want you to offer me friendship. I want you to seek God's face. And I want you to pray about it and have faith. I want you to lean on God totally for direction…"

"Are you a pastor?" she asked feebly and he laughed.

"You have such a good sense of humour. I like you"

"But you've not prayed about the 'little wife'?"

"Most of what I've been doing in the past one month is also praying about you"

"About me"

He moved to crouch in front of her and looked straight into her eyes. "I want you to marry me"

"Wow, you know how to hit it hard, don't you"

"Don't play modesty. You were expecting this proposal today, were you not?"

"Truth or dare?"

"Truth"

"I want to be your wife"

He burst into laughter and laughed for a long time. She joined in at first and then shook him and asked him to stop it.

"What? What's so funny?"

"Truth or dare"

"Dare"

"I dare you to deny it. You knew I was going to propose to you today"

"No"

"I dare you, girl. If I had not proposed, you would have done it your self" he said and they both laughed.

"Oh baby" he took her hands in his. "The Holy Spirit told me to buy the ring, said you would say yes but my faith couldn't hold that. It was too good to be true so I don't have a ring today poor me, but my heart I place in your hands today. I want you to love me as I love you. I want you to help me as God created you to, and most importantly, I want us to have a life together" he bent and kissed the back of her hand.

"Yes, I will, my love".

God still arranges good love stories. People still fall in love without knowing themselves before. And there is still something called, 'falling in love'. These days we have many literatures that give you the 101 basics of falling in love. I must say that these books, though very informative and helpful, sometimes take the light out of falling in love. At the end, a brother or a sister is left confused about what falling in love is really like. And some say they are in love with two or three people. And I ask myself, is it really possible to be 'in love' with more than one person? The way I see it is that, you 'love' someone for what they are or have but you are not 'in love' with the person. When you are 'in love', it's hard to describe what you feel. You can't even say the real reason you love the person; you just realise this person works for me! I feel good with this person. A vacuum is created when this person is not around, and it's just a plain, complicated, warm, happy, sad feeling that can only just be complemented by that person. I have seen very quiet people 'light' up when the one they love is around. Hard guys become like babies, naughty people want to behave themselves, a talkative wants to be calm and controlled… it's awesome when a person is 'in love'. Life just is beautiful!

Have you discovered your true feelings yet? Please do. Your heart may not be in the hands of the most handsome or pretty of the bunch. He may not be the richest and she may not be the smartest but love is worth every while. I wish you the best discovery.

WISDOM FOR SINGLES

WHEN MAMA SAYS 'NO'

MAMA WAS THE PILLAR of the home. Quiet, but effective. All through Jabulani's growing up years, Mama had been the engaging force that kept the home together. Things had been rough but Mama had remained the rigid feature. At the time when his little sister, Mandisa had come home pregnant, it had been Mama who solidly supported her, while reconciling and melting the ice that settled over their home. All through the years of Kanelo's drug addiction and gangster-ism, Mama had been the shoulder everyone leaned on, including Papa. Everyone, over the years had leaned on Mama's wisdom and soft sternness. In every situation, she seemed to have a counsel, one that always saved the day.

When Jabulani met Mbhali, the first thought in his mind was what Mama would think. He had loved her at first sight, before knowing who she was, or where she was from. Her creamy complexion was rare, almost translucent. She had long, curly dark hair which she wound around her head in a high wrap, leaving tendrils that teased her slender neck. He had been in the bank, getting some cash and she had been working in one of the other counters away from him. He hadn't been able to keep his eyes away from her. Something which had never happened to him before. He had returned to the bank later to see and ask her out on a date. It took him consistent pestering of three months before she agreed to that first date.

When Jabulani told Mama about Mbhali, the first thing she said discouraged him totally.

"She can't be right for you"

"Mama, you don't even know her. She's a wonderful person"

"She's mixed. You said so yourself"

"Her mother is Indian, her father is Zulu. They are a very happy family. She's just what I need" he defended heatedly.

"Do you even know what you need?" Mama chuckled in mockery, annoying Jabulani.

"I'm thinking of bringing her home to meet you and Papa" he said.

"When on earth did you meet her? You don't bring anybody to our home, son, except the person you want to be married to" Mama said conclusively. Jabulani wanted to retort that he planned to marry Mbhali, but Mama waved him off, staunching any protests he had.

The stalemate continued for months. Jabulani loved Mbhali more, explaining to anyone that cared to listen why she was the right woman for him. Mama's reasons were all flimsy. At first, she complained about Mbhali's racial mix. Then she went on to complain about her profession. 'Why is she not a teacher or a doctor, or something? Why a bank clerk?' Jabulani had defended heatedly. Banking was a noble profession, as noble as teaching or even more! And as long as Mama refused to meet Mbhali, Jabulani tried to keep it a secret from her. He had spoken so highly of his mother to her that she was itching to meet the most important woman in Jabulani's life. After courting for a whole year, it became ridiculous that Jabulani's family had not yet met Mbhali, while her family had met him and were all in love with him. He had to confess his problem to her.

She was very understanding. "You know mothers are always very jealous over their sons" she said. "And you're the first"

"Yes, but nonetheless, she hasn't even met you!" he exclaimed.

"I'm sure we will connect, and soon shove you aside" she said, trying to make him feel better. "Tell you what, why don't we spring a surprise on her" she suggested.

"No, I don't think that's a good idea. Mama hates surprise visitors" he shook his head.

"Not if it's her first daughter-in-law" she said jovially. Jabulani did not think it was a good idea but he agreed. They chose Mama's birthday.

It was the worst mistake of their relationship. Mama bluntly refused to take the gift Mbhali brought. She replied statements posed to her tartly and announced publicly that her day had been ruined by Jabulani and his guest.

When Jabulani offered to take Mbhali home, she declined. She had never been so offended in her life.

"I guess we will never see each other again after tonight" she announced, sniffing.

"What do you mean by that?" Jabulani asked defensively.

"Just what it sounds like. Your mother wants you to choose between me and her. She calmly disapproves of me and not one of you tried to speak for me while she cleaned me off the surfaces of her house…"

"Com'on, Mbhali please. You are reading meaning into her actions"

"Like I expect you'll defend her"

"She was just shocked that's all. I told you she hates surprises…"

"No, she was thrilled when your brother came in, surprising everyone of us. That had not been her reaction the minute we walked in…"

"Look, don't make an issue out of this" Jabulani said impatiently. "Give it time"

"Is that all you have to say? You don't think she was wrong?" her voice shook.

"You don't understand her, she means no harm. If you don't want to see me again, say so. Don't use my mother as excuse!" he snapped and left her on the front steps of his house.

When he got in, Mama was waiting for him.

"Mama, not tonight" he walked off angrily.

Jabulani finally broke off his relationship with Mbhali, after announcing to his whole family, he would never marry any other woman. Not one single member of his family stood against Mama's opposition. Not even Papa.

Mothers usually have a strong hold on their children, especially, if over the years, she has been a role model, supportive, and full of wise counsel; as every good woman should be. However, you as an adult child of a good woman should know when to draw the line between being wise, full of counsel, support, her reputable intuition and what you want for your life, and your future. You are now grown up and what qualifies you to talk about marriage is that you are mature enough to talk about marriage. The Bible says that a 'man' will leave his mother and father and cleave to his 'wife'. It's for 'men' and 'women' not 'boys' and 'girls'. I do not undermine parental guidance and I believe in a mother's intuition but you have to know when to draw the line! Whether you like it or not, your mother is your past; your spouse is your future. Human beings do have their tendency to manipulate and dominate and even if you do not see your mother as such a person, she may have gotten a 'false' impression of who you are and what you want, and believe she is the best judge of what's good for you.

Many sons have made mistakes and missed the best wife they could have had. And many daughters have ended up with 'wife-beaters' and stingy men because Mama was so sure that 'guy' was their daughter's dream come true.

You have to come to stand on what you believe, and this is why it is so important to have a mind of your own! As a child of God, what God is saying comes before what Mama is saying! Or what Papa wants. Get that straight, and God will help you to make the right choice. Amen.

WISDOM FOR SINGLES

BREAK IT, DON'T FAKE IT!

SEVERAL TIMES JIBOLA HAD heard the saying, and believed it worked: Fake it till you make it! It was a principle he had applied to some other areas of his life. For instance, after listening to a motivational message in church, he had made it a point of duty not to buy inferior clothes for himself anymore, faking a wealth he could not even afford, till he made it affordable. It had worked. Now he drove a good car, and wore the kind of clothes he hadn't been able to afford some years earlier. For his love life, it didn't seem to be working.

When he met Fehinti, he had thought she was the most beautiful creature in the female species. And truly she was. He had worked with the planning committee of a Christian beauty pageant where she had contested and won! It wasn't the normal local competition that everyone seemed to be organising, it was a continental one. Christian beauties from all over Africa converged in Abuja for the competition. In fact, Fehinti represented Nigeria, out of over thirty African Queens. Her victory was sure; she was beautiful, confident and highly intelligent. Jibola approaching her for a relationship had been like the children of Israel stepping into the Red Sea before it parted.

He had discovered too late that she was in another relationship, but she liked him instantly and agreed to a date. He felt strange about it. Why would she accept to date him, when she wore another man's engagement ring? Still he went ahead with the relationship, seeing it a small victory when Fehinti broke off with the guy, to be with him. At the time, he had nothing. He was a simple hustler, fresh graduate, struggling to make ends meet, between odd jobs, one of which had led him to the beauty pageant. And then he got a job with a small car shop as a sales representative. It wasn't much but it was much better than anything he'd had before. Fehinti seemed disappointed by that and their relationship started spiralling downward.

Jibola didn't quite understand her grouch at first. Did she want him to be jobless all his life? Then he realised that she had hoped he would get a better job and not settle for such a job as a sales representative. He argued that the job had gotten him his own first car and she argued back that his car was ten times older than the brand new ones he marketed. She told him to get another job and when the pressure grew, he started a small scale business by the side, making and marketing shirts to his customers.

Suddenly, things didn't seem to flow as well as before. Trust became an issue between them. Once in a while, Jibola would inquire about Fehinti's plans, and get a cold shoulder. Initially, it was hard to notice because of Fehinti's itinerary as queen. Shortly after her reign as beauty queen, she travelled out of the country without letting him know. When she finally got back and he expressed his displeasure, she brushed him off.

"She wants you to end the relationship, bros" his friend, Akin told him.
"I love her. That's my problem" Jibola sighed.
"You think you love her. She's making you miserable. Soon she'll date another man and dump you"
"That, I don't know, but I don't think so. What we had, I mean have is so different. I…"
"You don't love her anymore"

"I love her, very deeply. She loves me too. It's just that this job of mine is standing between us. I'm working on getting another job"

"And if she doesn't like that too? Is job the priority in your relationship now?"

"Right now, I just wish I could go away for a long time. Just disappear"

"With her?" Akin teased.

Jibola flashed him a straight 'dagger'.

Fake it till you make it, and if you don't, break it! If it's not 'flowing' as before, why waste your time and your partner's? Marriage is not a child's play. The moment you start having cold feet, and suspecting the other person, deal with it. Many relationships suffer because one person is waiting for the other person to call it off. That is not right. The minute you start switching off, let your partner know how you feel. It's not right to pretend you love someone or you are not suspicious. Lay your cards on the table and free your mind.

It may not sound as easy as I make it out to look because your heart is involved here but if a break is imminent, the more you delay, the more painful it will be when you finally let it go. Examine your motives and your partner's. Revisit the foundation of your relationship. Did you break someone's heart to win your partner's? What did God tell you when you started? Are you just struggling because it will be shameful to you to leave that person?

No reason is good enough to be in a relationship with someone, if it is not genuine! Whatever other reason for staying with someone, defeats the very essence of love, marriage and godliness.

Please stop deceiving that person. No matter how painful it is, only the truth can make you free.

WISDOM FOR SINGLES

THE STRANGER

THE STRANGER WAS SUPPOSED to be exposed out of his hiding place but each time the scripture came across Ada, she cringed. She harboured her stranger and protected everything that concerned him. A stranger who had a name, a handsome face, a fat pocket and a great personality. A stranger called Chijioke. He was one stranger she made special effort to keep in hiding.

She had met Chijioke at a very unlikely place, the child dedication of her friends, Ngozi and Ebere's, baby. As one of the hostesses at the after-church party, Ada had walked up and down, attending to guests. Though she had noticed him in church because she was an usher, there was more to the attention she gave him. He was a sight to catch. He was tall, fair-skinned and dark-haired. And very handsome.

He sat at a table with some of Ebere's colleagues from the office. There was a lot of booze on their table and Chijioke lit a cigarette after the meal, but Ada couldn't see beyond the flashy 'Bobo'. Somehow, she got herself introduced, and somehow, one thing led to the other. She was in love with 'the forbidden fruit'. To make matters worse, he showered her with love and attention.

Initially, she fooled herself with the notion that she was in his life to change him but after preaching to him once, and receiving a rebuff, she dropped the idea. Then she tried to exonerate herself by believing that her lifestyle and 'quiet and godly conversation' would make a difference. When this failed, she dropped the whole idea and threw herself into loving him and making it work. And it did work as long as she continued to compromise. He made it clear to her that he was not the church type, though he feared God. He didn't want to be pressurized into serving God like a 'fanatic'. He also requested she allow him continue with his drinking and smoking – they were a complete part of his adult life he was not willing to relinquish. In exchange, he promised not to hinder her from serving God the way she wanted. They had a truce.

Apart from the compromises, they loved each other. Chijioke pampered her with gifts and expressed love for her.

The attention was great.
The gifts were enormous.
And the sex was constant!

Esau gave up his birthright for a plate of porridge and we go, ooh! What a shame? David slept with Bathsheba and then had her husband Uriah killed and we waoh and wonder, how could he? Judas betrayed Jesus for thirty pieces of silver and we call him the 'son of perdition'.

You sleep and compromise and mess around with unbelievers and you go, 'it's not easy!' 'she's so nice' 'I don't know how it happened' 'it's for a purpose' 'I know God understands'

STOP!

Just stop it because you have no excuse. The Bible asks this question and I want you to think it over and answer sincerely. In the book of Romans, what shall separate us from the love of God? Can the love of a man or the love of a woman do the trick? Ask yourself carefully, sincerely.

As long as you are with that person, you are selling your birthright and crucifying Jesus all over again, allowing his killers to spit in His face and yell at him.

Search yourself.

WISDOM for PASTORS

Pr 10:13 Wisdom is found on the lips of him who has understanding

Dedicated to my husband and Pastor:
Afolarin
A rare gift to the body of Christ

CONTENTS

WISDOM FOR PASTORS

PROLOGUE

PAUL TRIED TO CONCENTRATE on his message without looking at the right side of the pews. It was hard to avoid. It actually wasn't all of the right side. It was the back side of the right side. He stammered once and quickly looked into his notes. He said one or two things from it and broke into a chorus. It helped him to organise himself. The congregation flowed with him without noticing a thing but he couldn't get it out of his mind. From the moment he mounted the pulpit, he had seen the unmistakable face of Bishop Jose. What was he doing here? He breathed in and prematurely brought his sermon to an end. It occurred to him to recognise the presence of the great general but thought against it. Dressed as he was, sitting as he did, Paul guessed the man just wanted to be. As soon as he took his seat, he sent his PA to inquire from the great man of God and to fix an appointment.

Bishop Jose sat quietly in the back pew long after all the members of congregation had left, waiting patiently for Pastor Paul to finish with counselling and meetings. He had all day and the rest of his lifetime, to wait. He was no longer in a hurry. He had been waiting for three hours before Pastor Paul finally came out.

"I'm so sorry, sir. I had to rush over it and then send some away so that you'll not wait too long sir" Paul gushed. Bishop Jose allowed him to finish and looked into his eyes.

"You should never postpone God so man will not be kept waiting" Bishop replied and smiled. "Have a sit"

Paul sat uncomfortably.

"You are wondering about a lot right now, I guess?"

"Yes sir. I… I'm short of words"

"I decided to wait and visit you. I believe in you, your message was powerful and I want to share from my life and experience. I know you've probably heard about what happened to me. How I lost everything, wife, ministry, children…" his voice trailed off. Paul nodded, confused as to why the man would come to him. And don't tell me you got a dream and saw me in it…

"I won't" Bishop winked at him, knowingly.

"Sir…" Paul gasped.

"The gift and calling of God are without repentance. And I won't pretend I've lost the gift. I still embarrass people when I tell them what's going on in their minds" he sighed. "I don't know you. I never did. I wanted a small place to worship and walked in here" Bishop explained softly and wiped his face with a towel. "When you sent someone to inquire after me, I decided it could be worth the trouble of talking with you and sharing part of my lessons in life…"

"I am privileged sir. But first, I must invite you to lunch. And please don't say 'no'"

"I won't. I'm hungry. Where's your wife?"

"I am not yet married, sir"

"Hmmm. We have a lot to talk about then. Come let's go and eat, and I'll tell you things. Things my eyes have seen in ministry"

WHO DID THE CALLING: GOD OR MAN?

WHEN AMADI SIGNED THE acceptance letter in his hand, a lot more than ink on paper transpired in his life. He was taking a decision to switch destiny. After being a successful Information Technologist, he was finally succumbing to the call to serve in the full time. It was leaving the world of certainty for a life of uncertainty. His wife, Edna had accepted the fate with all humility. She had always seen him doing more for God.

The first thing they had done was move from Lagos to the capital of their home state, Portharcourt. Amadi had specifically told Edna this was where God wanted him to be relevant. During his years of working for himself, he had amassed enough wealth to sustain him and his family, and had built a beautiful house in Eliogbolo where he moved his family to. They joined the branch of their Lagos church recommended by their pastor.

Amadi had come with a letter of recommendation which would assist him in getting employed by the church. It wasn't much and he still went through the full procedure of getting employed. When he got the job of a full-time deacon, he was elated. He had pursued the job for almost six months.

Things went normally for the first few years. Amadi worked hard. His pastors were impressed by his zeal and commitment. Nothing was too small to do, and nothing was too big. His wife and children supported him fully. Though they had lived in affluence, none complained about the meagre stipend the church could afford. They adjusted to their new lifestyle, seeing it also as a service to God.

The first signs of strain began to show shortly after Amadi was appointed to assist a pastor over one of the branch churches. Some other pastors who'd been long in the system began to murmur and complain. They insinuated that Amadi was bribing his way to the top. One or two of them walked up to him and challenged him but his refute fell on deaf ears. Amadi suddenly found himself in turbulent waters.

Within a few months, the superintendent pastor who employed him was transferred out of the region and a new pastor was sent. In Amadi's words;
"A Pharaoh that knows not Joseph!"
This was the exact situation. First, Amadi's antagonists black-listed him to the new man. He was posted to another branch church to head the congregation but it was a much smaller church in Buguma, his home-town. The transfer meant his ten –year old son who was about finishing elementary school would have to either go to boarding school or finish up school in Buguma. It also meant his family would leave Portharcourt. Edna could not bear to do that so they reached a compromise: Edna stayed back with the children while Amadi travelled to see his family once every two weeks. The church was a brand new one and the members were just a handful. Much had to be done and Amadi sometimes couldn't make the bi-weekly visit. He complained a few times and got rebuked for loving home more than God.

Amadi worked hard at his new station, and God blessed his efforts. The church grew. The new superintendent visited during their first year anniversary and saw how far they had gone. Amadi had even secured a small but good piece of land for the church and they were set on building. As the pastor praised his efforts and encouraged him, Amadi reminded him of his request to get transferred back to Portharcourt or its environs.

"You have done very well and do deserve to be promoted" the superintendent said.

Amadi's promotion did come about six months later but to his utter amazement, it was an appointment in another church outside the state. He was sent to the river rine area of Delta State. Even though his status had been raised and his salary increased a little, the location was worse. Edna cried for days.

Amadi worked in that location for three hell-on-earth years. His family was almost breaking up from the confusion. Sometimes, he didn't get to go home for six to eight weeks at a stretch. The allowance he got was not enough to cater for his family. His eldest daughter who had gained admission into the university could not pay her fees, and had to look for a clerical job. The branch church was too small and poor and they couldn't help their pastor. Amadi applied to the regional headquarters for a loan and was refused on the grounds that loans were given only for ministry-related problems.

He was stranded. His family had cut off from him when he decided to go into full-time ministry. Edna's family had lent them money so many times and they'd never been able to pay back, he was ashamed to ask for their help again. His second daughter could not pay for the final examination in high school. His son, now fourteen was sent home because they couldn't pay the fees. Edna, who had since started a small buying-and-selling business, had depleted her capital. It was a crash they had seen coming for long.

Amadi shot up from his bed one early morning. He had not been home for over eight months but he knew the things that had been happening. His anointing was drained from constant crying and complaining. His church members could not even feed themselves, not to talk of helping him. He couldn't even 'borrow' from the church purse. There was nothing to borrow. The regional and national headquarters had not helped him despite all the calls for help.

Even God! Where was God? His family was in shambles. Edna had been forced to rent out the boys' quarters of their home to get a little more change! He, Amadi, who had controlled millions of naira managing his own IT firm! When he sold his controlling shares of the company, his partners had thought he was mad. Now he couldn't even eat two square meals! His family was in pieces. What had he done? Who called him? Was it really God, or his foolish exuberance?

Amadi shot up from his bed that morning without even saying a word of prayer. He packed his bags and went back home to Portharcourt. Edna screamed when she opened the door to him.

"I'm back home" he said flatly. "We are starting our own church, here. In this city. In this house!"

"Amadi was successful in his church. He still has a church till today. I met him at a conference in California. He was a faculty member at a seminar for pastors. He spoke on church priorities" Bishop Jose said.

"Sir, would you say it was God who called him to start his own church?" Paul asked, confused.

"You are pastoring for someone aren't you?" Bishop counter-asked.

"Yes sir, I am"

"Are you happy doing what you are doing?"

"I am sir. I am fulfilled. I am doing exactly what I always believed God wanted me to do"

"Then stick to it. Many pastors confuse the calling of God with their talent and desire. The fact that you can preach well does not mean you must pastor. Remember Amadi said God was calling him to work in Portharcourt. He sold his company to go to Portharcourt and then left all that to go into interior villages where he had no conviction to work. His spirit repelled it from the start. How was God expected to do anything through him like that?"

"But what about spiritual authority? Are we not supposed to obey those in authority? Those who have rule over us?" Paul asked heatedly.

"You are supposed to obey spiritual authority. But let me ask you? Who called you?"

"But God ordained all leadership. He permitted them to be over me"

"He did. But if you need to move and you don't, who's to blame? Don't box God with your theology son. If you were never in the right place at the first, will you argue about spiritual authority? That authority isn't even meant to be over you in the first place. And then if God says time to move and you don't, where does that leave you? But I don't agree with leaving anyhow. Leave right. Leave well. Don't poison people's minds. But you need to discern, son"

"You're right, sir" Paul mumbled.

"Let me ask you this question: is it every gift they give you that you receive?"

"Gift?"

"Yes, just like, is it everywhere they send you to pastor that you go?"

"I guess"

WISDOM FOR PASTORS

SANCTIFY THE SINNER'S GIFT

THE WEATHER WAS FAVOURABLE for everyone that day. The crusade had been more successful than Akello or any of the pastors could believe. God was indeed faithful. Souls were won to the kingdom in numbers. Akello was grateful to God. The village of Ntusi had experienced the revival like never before. Akello had even spotted a couple of foreign archaeologists working on the mounds in and around the village. Now he could go for his vacation with his family, rest-assured that all was well.

Akello was a pastor over a small congregation. Small by his own standards but by no means small amongst his colleagues. He had started the church with the full support of his beautiful wife, Sanyu, in the heart of Ntusi, a few miles away from Kampala. His friends had told him to move into the city where success would be instantaneous. If he didn't want Kampala, why not Jinja with all the industrial prospects or even Mubende. Some of them had taken the choice, setting up big churches where they were sure the tithes would be big and the offerings, fat. Akello stuck to Ntusi. And God blessed him there. He proved to all his friends who had 'copper miners' and 'sugar plantation owners' members, wrong. God could make nothing from something. Even in Ntusi, God could make his life better than those of his counterparts in Kampala, Jinja, and other major cities.

But despite his success and joy, Akello was not content with his level. Yes, he knew there were still greater exploits ahead but even at this point, he expected more. More commitment from his leaders and members: commitment financially, and all otherwise. The worst part was that he didn't realise that until it was late. So when Mwaka joined the church, it wasn't anything new. Mwaka told everyone he had worked with a multinational company in Kampala for a while before relocating to Ntusi. He spoke little of his life before Ntusi and no matter how close anyone got to him, no one knew much about him.

He was however a departure from what Akello had been used to. He was committed to the church and his pastor. Akello noticed him the first time when they had a guest minister come from Entebbe. Mwaka single-handedly fed the preacher for four days. It wasn't much anyway until he single-handedly bought a drum-set for the church. Akello thanked God for the ministry gift. Gradually, Mwaka's relevance to the church became a landmark. He was always there doing things for God. He was sponsoring programmes, paying bills, changing everything from offering envelopes, to pastor's car!

Akello was still in vacation when the call came in from one of his elders. Mwaka was arrested and Pastor was needed for questioning because his name had been mentioned as a beneficiary. Akello was shocked. Never in his life had he been so humiliated. Straight out of vacation, Akello went into police custody. He was detained for three days through which time he was interrogated vigorously. He was released on bail after the third day.

The police listed items Mwaka had given to the church over a period of one year. It amounted to almost eighty million Ugandan shillings. Amongst other things, he had purchased a large parcel of land for the church, a utility van and given large donations to support welfare projects. Mwaka was actually a wanted rogue, an accountant who had swindled his company in excess of five hundred million Ugandan shillings.

Akello realised he never even knew what sort of business his devout member was in to.

Paul sat dumbfounded for a few seconds after Bishop Jose had kept quiet.

"I know what you are thinking" Bishop said. "Akello didn't deserve that, right?"

"Well sir, maybe he deserved it. Maybe he was careless"

"Ha, I got you wrong then. But what could he have done? Mwaka was a relief to his pastor and the church"

"Such a relief, sir. Such a suspicious relief"

"So you would not accept gifts a person wants to give to his God?" Bishop asked teasingly.

"The problem is sir; I have such a person in my church right now. I'm afraid of his source but he's such a…" Paul paused.

"A relief" Bishop said.

"What do I do?" Paul groaned.

"Stop him!"

"Stop him? How? Do I tell him not to give?"

"Tell him to reduce his giving. Tell him to save his money"

"Sometimes he just pays directly to the church account and then sends the teller" Paul shook his head, "What if he is genuine? Besides, we need what he is giving so badly. Can't I just receive the gift with a pure heart without suspecting…?"

"Like sanctifying the gift and ignoring the giver?" Bishop laughed. "No, I don't think so. You see, the fact that you are suspicious means there is cause to be suspicious. You have to check it out. He is your member. You have spiritual authority over him so you should call him and explain to him that you are not comfortable with his source of income. You want to know everything. To help you, take one of your leaders with you, one who feels the same about this. He will be your witness"

"What if gets offended and he leaves or stops giving and he is genuine?" Paul exclaimed.

STAY

AKELLO HAD SPENT THREE days in police detention. His car had been impounded by the police; the church land and even the personal land he bought for himself with his money at about that same period, confiscated; equipments from the church had been auctioned off; most of all, he had been badly defamed. In the cosy society of Ntusi, he made small-talk. All the success of the crusade washed down the drain. A few of his friends began to avoid him. Some openly criticized him. They accused him of dragging the name of the Lord in the mud.

Akello was devastated. It was as if the wind had just left his sail. His church membership dropped by half. His landlord sent him a quit notice. To crown his persecution, the church board met and placed him on a three-month suspension. The only one who stood by him was Sanyu, and she faced as much persecution as her husband. The gossips had a field's day murmuring. Everywhere they turned in the village, they heard something. People called them names. Akello thought of only one thing to do, leave Ntusi. He decided to move his family to his uncle's house in Entebbe while he stayed with a friend in Jinja for the space of the three months he would be on suspension.

He felt he had been unjustly treated. He had reported himself to his father-in-ministry in Kampala but word had already reached the bishop. And the father was very angry with the son! The question the few people who bothered to give him a chance to defend himself asked was: did you not look at him? Do you sincerely think the guy was making the kind of money he was giving you? The answer was obvious. In that regard, Akello knew he had ignored the gnawing voice of reason. He had silenced every voice in his head. And that was his only offence.

Feeling alone and tired of the sudden turn in his fortune, he sent his family to Entebbe. The day after, he was in his house, packing up his luggage and a few other essentials, knowing in his heart he would probably not come back, when his phone rang. There was almost nothing left for him. Years of sweat and hard work had just been washed down the drain by one simple mistake. One day he was up, bubbling and rejoicing, the next he was completely out of the picture; left in the cold with no friend and no family.

It was his good friend in Jinja, Pastor Able.

"I have good news for you, I fixed a meeting for you and it will hold in the community hall. I was lucky to get it at the price I did" Pastor Able said.

"Yeah, thanks" Akello said without enthusiasm.

"You don't sound excited"

"I can't be. I'm not even sure I should start having any meetings now"

"You need the money. And you need to prove to everybody the anointing is without repentance" Able said softly. He was the only one who offered to help Akello back on his feet and that was saying a lot because Akello had been popular among pastors.

"Are we even sure people will attend?"

"I don't like this spirit. Listen to me; you are out of your church now. This is the time to start over. You've got to get this behind you and start over. See, my Bishop always says that don't stay where you are tolerated, go where you are celebrated…"

"Your bishop has all the rhymes doesn't he?" Akello chuckled.

"He's right. They don't appreciate you in Ntusi. I always told you. Come over to Jinja and start over. By the time the suspension period is over, you send in your resignation. That's close to three months. I'm offering to help you start up here. How many pastors will want you to come to their territory to set up something" Able argued.

"As far away from you as Ntusi is, some pastors still feel I'm too close for comfort" Akello sighed.

"That's exactly what I'm saying. Take advantage of the anointing of God on your life, man of God" Able insisted.

"Well, I'm already packing my bag. I'll be with you before nightfall" Akello said.

"Great. You can rest and use tomorrow to prepare. Day after, the meetings start. We'll talk about sharing the expenses when you arrive"

"Sure" Akello mumbled.

"We will do great things together in this city, brother. We will take over the land, for Jesus" Able said excitedly.

"I don't think his decision was alright. He didn't leave right did he?" Paul wondered.

"That's not the question. The question is still back to where we started from. Who asked him to leave?"

"Pastors like doctors, find it hard to swallow their own pill"

"You get my drift, son. Akello will suspend his members like we all do. Fornication, theft, greed, misconduct, you name it. We are quick to mete discipline but we can't imagine the humiliation of serving 'time'. What is so bad in staying out your punishment and moving on from there? You see, what we don't realise is that when we run from correction; we will keep running from the correction. You will make that mistake again and if you don't pay your dues, you will keep falling prey. I encouraged my members to face the music when they form the choir. If you have done something wrong, stay and serve your punishment. Learn from your mistakes and move on from there. Your anointing is without repentance but it is not an occasion for you to sin. The Bible says in Rom.6:1, should we continue in sin so that grace may abound? God forbid! There is joy in discipline. God says that the one He loves He chastises. If God leaves you to your own, it means you are not important to Him. The same way if you offend and it does not make the evening news, then you are in trouble! That means you are a perpetual sinner. People don't appreciate your ministry. The devil should appreciate your ministry and rejoice over your downfall… so what are we saying here? What do you expect if you fall into error? People should talk! The devil should rejoice! Your friends should back down! Your elders should be disappointed! Nothing happened to Akello that wasn't supposed to happen. There was no reason to plan to leave. The bible even helps to excuse our faults, encouraging us to embrace failure with a right attitude, when it says 'the righteous fall seven time BUT', and that is where lies the victory, BUT he rises again. If you fall and crawl into hiding and from there run away, how does the devil know you made it back? How do your antagonists face you? Stay and deal with issues. And all that talk about being tolerated or being celebrated is completely out of context. You need a good dose of people tolerating you in life and ministry. Life is not a bed of roses. If you have to endure people's tolerance, aren't you lucky. Some people can't endure tolerance and that's why they run helter-skelter, looking for where they will be celebrated. Isn't it sweeter if you are celebrated in the same place you were tolerated? Listen, we pastors like to say rhymes that confuse the people we are leading. We use our position of influence to the detriment and progress of God's work…

"It has always puzzled me, sir. Why do we like to do that?"

"It's all about power. Sometimes we don't even know we are harming the person we are trying to counsel. I'll tell you the story of Adofo. I met him in Ghana when I went to establish my churches".

WISDOM FOR PASTORS

PASTOR NOT GOD

ADOFO WAS A VIBRANT young prophet on heat for God. Shortly after he gave his life to God, he discovered the gift of prophecy on his life and luckily for him, had a pastor who believed in helping the younger generation. His pastor Kofi, permitted him on several occasions to manifest his gifts and calling in the church. He went about with the man of God, ministering, edifying the body of Christ. There was such a bond between father and son.

One day, Adofo told his pastor that he wanted to enter a covenant of bond-servitude with him.

"I want to serve under you for the rest of my life" Adofo said. "My wife, my children will all be your servants in the ministry. Anywhere you ask us to go and anything you ask us to do, we will"

"This is such a heavy statement you make, Prophet Adofo" Pastor Kofi said. "Not only is it heavy for you, it is also very heavy for me and I want to pray about it"

"Yes sir. Thank you Daddy"

Kofi prayed about the issue and told Adofo the following day he believed there was going to be such a relationship between them and so, Adofo became Kofi's bond servant. To seal the bond, they went on a seven-day prayer and fasting.

Though the church was a large one and Adofo was already a paid staff, Kofi decided not to announce the bond in church. But he embarked on an important mission; getting Adofo a wife. With the backdrop of their relationship, he knew he had to be careful. His wife had to be someone agreeable and humble; someone who believed in the vision of the church. After discussing with Adofo, and his wife, he found three ladies that fitted the description; one of them even added an attribute, she was very beautiful.

- Mardea was a member of the choir, and was one of the oldest members of the church. She had come to church with her mother as a child when the church first started and had grown to be a willing and committed member. But further investigation also revealed she was in a relationship with one of the younger ministers. Kofi remembered after considering her that they had come to him to pray for them. Mardea was out.

- Panyin was an usher in the church. She had a twin brother who was a strong member of another church but that was not too much against her. She worked as a school teacher and was everything Adofo would need as a wife.

- Adwoa was the last of the three. She was a very beautiful girl, the most beautiful of the three, and a member of the prayer band.

After dismissing Mardea, Kofi asked Adofo to pray about the other two sisters. Adofo did not waste time with his reply, he was sure of who God speaking to him about.

Adwoa.

She was beautiful, from a very good Christian family, and her intercessory ministry would complement his prophetic, perfectly. There was no doubt in Adofo's mind. Neither was there in Kofi's mind. Until Adwoa was summoned into Kofi's office. After exchanging pleasantries, Kofi told Adwoa of his belief that she and Adofo were made for one another.

"He's a pastor sir…"

"A prophet by call" Kofi corrected her.

"Pastor, I don't see us together" Adwoa blurted out.

"Why would you say that?" Kofi asked, shocked.

"I know what I want in my husband and I just know Prophet Adofo is not it"

"I'm curious" Kofi murmured.

"He'll be tall and dark definitely…"

"Like Adofo" Kofi nodded.

"He's in the medical profession; nurse, doctor, pharmacist… whichever. And he is not a member of our church" she said confidently.

"Then there is someone" Kofi said, alarmed.

"There's no one… yet! But he will fit all of the descriptions. Adofo is tall and handsome and that's all to his credit. I really don't see us getting together" she said dismissively. Her bluntness confused Kofi. She sounded so sure.

"If there's no one for certain, then won't you even pray about this man of God? I am your pastor and I know what's good for you, child" Kofi said authoritatively. Probably to intimidate her!

"Yes Pastor. I know and I understand. And I thank you very much because I know you want the best for me. But you are my pastor, not my God" she said softly, careful not to offend him.

"There's nothing as irritating as a stubborn member" Paul said.

"Or an imposing pastor?" Bishop Jose asked.

Paul shook his head vehemently. "So what happened?"

"Adwoa left the church. Adofo married someone else entirely"

"I bet he is happy"

"I don't know. What I know is Pastor Kofi raised a lot of dust when she refused the relationship. He was so sure she was just being rebellious.

He suspended her for every little thing she did and antagonised her continuously. At the end, she left"

"Good for everyone"

"But you are not God are you? Because of your own personal conviction, you send a good member out of the church. I have seen pastors arrange relationships that flop wickedly. I feel bad about it but my youth pastor married my first daughter. I arranged it. They both consented because of their mutual respect for me and because I subtly threatened them. Today, that marriage is still a thorn in my flesh. I didn't give them a chance to refuse and they were not strong enough to stand against me. Listen, we pastors like to assume the position of God in the lives of those under us. Because God gives us the privilege of overseeing his people, we begin to forget that we are servants of servants. Just so that you'll sound right, you cannot lord it over anyone. We use our position to impose transfers and gifts and relationships. People have their lives to live…"

"But it is the place of the pastor to lead and direct and stop the sheep from going astray" Paul argued.

"To lead and direct and help to prevent the sheep from going astray but you do know an African proverb says a dog that wants to get lost will never hear the whistle of his master. We are caretakers. We are servants. We lead by love not force. We give directions not order. We appeal, not impose. We obey the master no matter what the outcome is. We are not to birth destinies; we are to mid-wife and attend to destinies birthed by the spirit of God. Learn son, so you won't face the bitter consequence"

WISDOM FOR PASTORS

WE ARE FLESH AND BLOOD

Azubuike rushed into the bathroom adjoining his office and splashed cold water on his face. The small space he used as an office suddenly became like prison walls, closing in on him. He blew a few tongues and breathed deeply. He wondered where everyone was and why he would be faced with such a dreadful experience so early in the day, early in the year!

"I plead the blood of Jesus" he sighed. He leaned back against the wall and covered his face with his two hands. "God, I'm sorry" he murmured. A voice in his head shouted, but for what? "I don't know. I'm just so sorry". Drips of water fell on his shirt front and he looked at it as though it was blood. You did nothing wrong, the voice in his head insisted.

"I did nothing wrong, for now" Azubuike said to himself and walked slowly back into his office. As soon as he sat down, his eyes caught sight of the small brown envelope under his table. "For now" he reminded himself. "As long as I don't touch the money, I'm okay" he kept his eyes to the floor. It's a gift. Only a gift. The gift of a man makes room. If they need a favour from you, a gift can pave the way for the favour. It's just like sowing a seed toward a blessing. It's what you preach everyday!

"It can't be right" Azubuike thought aloud. But this is a blessing. You need the money. Your wife is going to deliver any day now. What if it is a caesarean section? Do you ask the church to finance that too? It could roll into hundreds of thousands of naira if you use the right hospital. You deserve the best. You need this money. It is your due. This is what the bible means when it says you reap where you sow. If you work in the vineyard, you should eat from the vineyard. This is what it means, the voice in his head cried insistently.

"That's not what it means, Zubby, and you know it" he said to himself. His head dropped into his hands and he scratched his scalp. It's true he needed the money. Though it was just fifty thousand naira, it would go a long way. He should be more than this money, he thought. Fifty thousand should not be enough to sway him at this level but despite his position as a regional coordinator, his office was small and sparsely furnished. Besides, all the power he had lay in this little office. He was no longer pastor over a congregation! Despite all his anointing, he had been promoted to this purely administrative seat! Once in a while, a church invited him to preach in their special program. Like once in four months. They all dreaded inviting him because they would have to 'load his boot' with gifts. The bigger churches who could afford that, could also afford inviting bigger ministers from other ministries and so they avoided him and went for the big bishops. He was caught between a strait. Though the headquarters catered for all his needs; it was just in the written agreement. In reality, he couldn't bring himself to state all his needs. For instance, the kind of hospital he deserved to take his wife for delivery. The church would sponsor the general hospital or the teaching hospital but he would prefer a private hospital; those ones that charged as though they were hotels. Where they served three-course meals to their patients! He had visited a member there once before he got his 'promotion'.

Fifty thousand naira could sway him. In this present day Nigeria, even fifty thousand naira could wake a dead man. He picked the money and looked into the envelope. It was packed in three bundles, two two-hundred naira bills, and one one-hundred naira bundle. He touched the money gently, as though afraid to wake a sleeping child.

"Even God knows I deserve this money" he whispered. It was a bribe. No need to white-paint a sepulchre. He had to decide what to do with it. The two men who had come into his office had stated their intentions clearly. They understood he was chairman of the reorganization committee for the year, a position he just received the day before. They wanted him to post them to favourable and buoyant churches in the next few months during the annual redeployment season. They had promised they would invite him to preach on their pulpits often and to seal their commitment to him, dropped the brown envelop. It was OH-HA, no beating about the bush. He wanted all of it. But what would he do? Had he been reduced to taking bribes? This had never happened to him before. Should he take the bribe and still go ahead and redeploy based on merit? Or should he just return the bribe. He had never met the two young men before, but he knew them by reason of their church locations. They seemed to have potential. And to crown it all, they had even invited him to their present churches. Though the churches were not too big, that was two invitations within the month! They would 'load his boot' Twice in one month!

"Isn't this like selling one's soul for a piece of bread?" he asked the empty room.

When he looked round his office again, his mind was made up. He would do what he would do to prove a point. He was in need! And someone somewhere had to hear it, even if it is a slap in their face.

Even if it is 'Baba' God Himself!

"I chipped in that account to show you we are human beings. Temptation does not look at face! In fact, when temptation decides to look at faces, he chooses the faces that are shining with God's glory first. We are flesh and blood and we are bound to fall if we are not careful. Azubuike was a big man in his church. Fifty thousand naira only, made him compromise. Can you imagine? Less than five hundred American dollars, and he's trying to prove a point; to who? I have often wondered the ways of men. Pastors especially believe they have the sole right of proving points! Because they believe it's from the mouth of the pastor to the ears of God! Sure, it is meant to be. We are the high priests. We are middle-men. God respects us. He respects our counsel. We are his spokesmen in a changing world but listen to me; we are also flesh and blood and should never forget that. The moment that realisation begins to slip, we begin to lose it. We begin to imagine sole proprietorship of the souls of saints. We begin to act unnaturally because we are, and yes we are spirit beings. But we are spirit beings living in the flesh in the now. Don't get me wrong, we should carry and compose ourselves as people being used of God. Just don't forget that children of God are exactly that. They are God's children and they can feel what you feel; know some of what you know and maybe more. And you are also vulnerable to making mistakes. When you carry yourself so high, when the fall comes, it may crush you. Your crash may not be caused by money.

"It can be with women, money, pride or ego; it can be a compromise or a sentimental judgement. It can become a deception or a lie. Many pastors live a false life. Like empty barrels making a lot of noise. They don't even know they've lost it! Now if that kind of pastor starts to lord it over you, what would you do? If you don't have a mind of your own, if you can't hear from God; like Berean Christians who know better…

"Paul, let's go to your house. I'm famished. We can talk more after a meal" he stood up and stretched.

THE WAY JESUS CALLED HIS DISCIPLES

THE LIFE OF AKELLO was such an interesting read, everyone around him came and took their fill of it. And like a book, you feed from it, and leave. You don't add your contribution to the publication. Akello's friends learnt from him and gave nothing in return.

Just as Pastor Able, his friend in Jinja had promised, he was received well. He settled in quickly and within a few months, brought in his family to join him. The church at Ntusi sent messages to him but he insisted he needed the time out to sort himself out. Even after the three months suspension period elapsed, he stayed back at Jinja. Ministry was easier. The pastors accommodated him, inviting him to preach in their churches. The few that were initially sceptical began to open up. Soon Akello's gift and calling was making waves for him. Pastor Able's church began to experience significant growth as a result of Akello's ministry gifting and anointing.

One day, after waiting on the Lord, Akello had a strong leading to start his own church in Jinja. He confided it to his wife who insisted they return to Ntusi, if they must head a church again. Her argument was simple.

"Pastor Able and all his friends will think we came to steal from them" she argued heatedly. "They will think it was all a plot to take all their members. They will never accept that God is calling you to start a work here"

"After all these months and years? I've invested weeks and days of tireless toil in this land. The increase many of them enjoy is as a result of the fasting and praying I invested into my programmes. Yes they gave me their pulpits and a platform to manifest but for goodness' sake, if they had not, would I still not have had a platform? Did they send me or God?"

Sanyu was devastated. "Please husband" she addressed him the way she did when she had an important point to make. "Please hear me out. Let us go to Entebbe or Kampala, Mubende, anywhere else. Not here. Not now"

"Pray about this as a good wife. Let me know what you hear from God" Akello said dismissively.

"I cannot pray about this, my love. I will only be deceiving myself. My mind is made up. I don't want us to start a church here. Nonetheless, you are the husband; you are the man, the head. And you are the pastor. You have the call. Anywhere you go, I will. Your God remains mine" she said softly, close to tears.

"Thanks for remembering" he said stiffly.

Akello held a power crusade in Pastor Able's church and being led of God, raised a special offering. The offering was tied to a special 30-day miracle and people gave their all. The proceeds from this offering were taken by Akello and he told his friend Able, that God had special need for the money so the miracle could be complete. With the money, he paid for a utility hall. He paid for handbills and public paid announcements.

This is how his friends knew he was starting his church!

Pastor Able almost went crazy. A few of the other pastors called him, confused and angry. He was just as miffed as they were. When he tried to call his friend's phone, it was switched off. Sanyu's number went through and she calmly apologised for their secrecy.

"We were afraid you would feel this way" she lied. "We really are sorry but it's what God seems to want for now"

"Where's your husband?" Pastor Able blasted, not having any of what she had to say.

"He's on a retreat. He won't be available till Sunday morning…"

"When the church starts. Neat arrangement" Pastor Able said angrily and hung up. Sanyu turned to her husband where he sat beside her, reading his Bible.

"If we will do whatever we plan to do, please let's do it right' she said softly.

"Don't start with me, please. What's the grouch this time?"

"Don't call anybody. Don't ask anybody to follow you, to leave their church…"

"Please stop this, Sanyu!" Akello exclaimed angrily. "How did Jesus get his disciples? Was it by kneeling and praying? Or waiting in the church hall for them to come? Get thee behind me, woman!" he stood up and stomped out of the room.

On Sunday morning, Pastor Able's church was lean. Almost all the financially buoyant members were not in church. He dreaded the worst. Service went normally but his heart was heavy and it was obvious why.

"Don't go" his wife said to him in the car as he swore he was going to tear up the service in Akello's church.

"I am not only going, we are going" he put the car in gear, and sped away in the direction of the utility hall where Akello had hired.

"You will only break your heart" his wife mumbled.

As it was, their hearts were both broken beyond repairs. When they got to Akello's church service, the parking lot was full to the brim. Thanksgiving offering was being taken and there was a lot of noise and rejoicing; singing and dancing.

"Oh my God!" Pastor Able screamed. "He has finished me"

"That is Dr. Edward's jeep. He single-handedly bought the land for church building last year" his wife gasped.

"He told me in confidence that before the end of this year, he would make sure he starts the building, and he wants us to move in before the end of next year. What's going to happen now?"

They sat mute in their car, willing themselves to move but unable to. They sat there till the service closed. They sat there till the members; their members began to file out, chatting and smiling. They sat still as some passed by their car; the sugar plantation owner, the bank manager and his family, the university don who just joined the church, several professionals from all walks of life, the medical doctors and their families, numbering four different families. They sat mute as these people passed, recognised them, and walked away quickly.

"Correct me if I am wrong sir, but is there any account where it was mentioned that Jesus scattered other people's flocks to gather his own?" Paul asked appalled.

"I can't recall, but his disciples must have had some religious bias before he called them, don't you think?" Bishop Jose picked his teeth. "The food was nice, by the way. A good cook, a good pastor"

"Thank you sir. All I need now is a good wife"

"Take your time. I'll tell you why. Later"

"I will be very upset if my friend treats me the way Akello treated his friends"

"His friends were all very upset. But that's what we do to ourselves. We give all sorts of rowdy excuses, crucifying Jesus all over again. Betraying him, and denying him, yet, we say it is all for him! The end does not always justify the means. Jesus never caused a friction in his own camp. Yes, the

Pharisees and Saducees and hypocrites, and the camp of the enemy all had it tough but you don't bite the hand that feeds you. You don't despise your friends. But many pastors do this. As soon as you find your feet, you wage the war against your own allies. There is a big problem with unity amongst believers and it is foul attitudes like this one that causes it. Don't twist the words and actions of Jesus to suit you. There is a curse attached to anyone that blasphemes the scriptures"

WISDOM FOR PASTORS

PROTECTING YOUR TERRITORY

PASTOR ABLE HAD BEEN in ministry for almost twenty-five years and had never seen this kind of confusion in all his years. Suddenly, he was faced with building from scratch, what he had almost brought to a peak. His high walls were suddenly flat on the ground. His worst fears realised at the hands of his closest ally. He now knew exactly how scriptural David felt being betrayed by his own brother.

Week after week, he tortured himself with the reality of all that had happened. In it all, he learnt one bitter lesson, not to trust anyone. As he came to this realisation, he set out with the vigour to make his point. His congregation had gradually thinned out to an elder and his family, and a few university students. He could hardly fill the front few pews of his church. He saw himself as having nothing to lose. Able launched out the age-long attack of exposing your enemy in defence of your territory!

His messages took a drastic turn. He studied books of the Old Testament and preached extensively and strategies of war. His message rallied around watching out for the enemy; destroying your enemies and taking over the possessions of the enemy. He did not spare his words. Anywhere Able went to preach, he openly scorned and disdained his friend, Akello. He specifically instructed his few old members, and the few new ones, to steer clear of the charismatic leader.

"He is self-destructive! Whatever a man sows, the same shall he reap" he bellowed in one of the Sunday services.

About three years after the whole incidence, Able had finally built a church and was almost back on track, Akello walked into his office. The two had not seen themselves 'eyeball-to-eyeball' since Akello left and Able's new secretary unknowingly ushered the 'big' man of God into the waiting room, excitedly running into the office to inform her boss of the valued visitor. His reply shocked her!

"Send him out of my office!" Able screamed, jumping out of his chair. The middle-aged woman shrank back in astonishment. "I mean no offence but that is the man who single-handedly stole twenty years of ministry sweat from me!" he said huskily.

"No one can blame Pastor Able. What would you do sir, if you were the one?"

"Let me tell you that I have been on the receiving end of this aggression before. Several times. It's not fun to be the traitor. It's like swimming against the tides…"

"But you caused it. You brought it upon yourself. Backstabbing cannot be condoned in the kingdom" Paul argued heatedly.

"Jesus was backstabbed. Almost all the kings and prophets experienced one form of betrayal or the other but it is not a good excuse to commit sin. I had a friend who said the only army that does not care for its wounded soldiers is the Christian army. What do we do to our offenders, we kill them. When our brothers make mistakes, we denounce them. Yes, Akello was horrid. He did the abominable. He hit his brother below the belt, but what does the brother do, he hits back!"

"In defence" Paul mumbled.

"No. He hits back in anger and bitterness and because the reward of his brother is not in his hands, he hits air! Killing your enemy is not going to make them go away. Even if they die physically or go on transfer, or they travel, enemy camp is always a part of a Christian life. You protect your territory from the enemy not from your allies, no matter how bad things turn out. It's hard and painful but I have not seen in scriptures where Jesus or any of the patriarchs antagonised one another the way we do today. My church seems to be so much more important than yours that we pastors now have the boldness to ban other pastors from ministering to the people of God. It's all an act of pain, anger, bitterness and malice and that definitely is not of God. Encourage your sheep to graze within the pasture. If the other shepherd does not forbid them, let them feed. You don't have everything it takes to win a soul; your brother has a part too. Don't constrain your members from feeding where the grass is green"

"Some members stray from church to church all the time. They are tossed to and fro. Should a good pastor not caution such a one?" Paul asked.

"Caution, don't cage! As painful as it may seem, let God fight your personal battles for you, your duty is to face the enemy. Spoiling another man's ministry gets you nowhere, definitely not to heaven. Bad-mouthing couldn't attract any reward from God either. If a man of God is true and genuine and can be a blessing to your flock, and is willing to be, why make policies that keep him away? Your policies and laws constrict and hinder progress. Just like the law keeps us in bondage, grace gives us freedom. If you have too many laws in your church, your members are in bondage. You cannot turn yourself into the Holy Spirit. That's why the presence of God has departed from many churches; the pastors have turned themselves into the Holy Spirit. They must see everything and make sure they hand-carry their members to heaven. You are destroying yourself and your member. Why do you think God said vengeance is His? Learn from the example of Abraham and Lot. Abraham allowed Lot to pick first! Let that pastor take his pick. Let him choose the best out of the sweat of your face. Then when he is gone, look up to heaven and receive instruction from your maker. It won't take you three years before your enemy comes running to seek forgiveness" Bishop Jose nodded in conviction. "I have seen it happen".

WISDOM FOR PASTORS

PASTORS' TETE-A-TETE

THE CHURCH GREW LIKE wildfire. Word spread round that God had finally gotten an office open 24/7. It was in Pastor Yemi's church. Within the first year, they had acquired a massive piece of land. Things were happening really fast. By the end of the second quarter of the second year, their building was sitting erect in a choice location at New Bodija, in the ancient city of Ibadan. The church members started work on the pastor's house. If anything, backbiters and that clique of people Pastor Yemi referred to as 'Tobiases', were shutting their mouths for a change.

"We are beginning to breathe fresh air" he told his ministers at the weekly meeting they held to plan and launch out.

Indeed, it was a breath of fresh air. When Yemi started the church, it had been tumultuous. He had started off as a pastor under a large ministry. Initially, they started in Ondo town and then began spreading all over the Western states of Nigeria. They targeted the state capitals. From Akure, they opened up at Ado-Ekiti, then Oshogbo. When the church moved to Oyo state, they needed a highly charismatic pastor who could pool the crowd. He had to be highly anointed also and an orator. Yemi stood out like a sore thumb! Even though he had only recently joined the church, he was already loved by everyone. The General Overseer sent him to Ibadan!

In Ibadan, Yemi did not live below expectations. He did massive evangelisms and worked harder than was rationally human. But he was not deterred. He was more determined than anyone else to make a mark, especially because he was the youngest amongst all the pastors. Many people had doubted his ability; many tried to discourage the G.O. the stakes were high on him, and he didn't want to let the people who believed in him down.

The church grew big after only six months but Yemi got a promotion that was least flattering. He was sent to Oshogbo which though an older church, was much smaller than Ibadan. He took it in good faith though with a lot of bitterness. He had served in Oshogbo for only three months when the church attendance blew up. To compliment Yemi, he got posted to the new church recently opened in Abeokuta which was having a small problem. Yemi went, but by now, the bitterness within him made him begin his own ulterior plans. He now realised the leadership of the church was 'using' him without any consideration for him. His wife who was not earning a living was complaining bitterly about the sudden and inconsiderate movements. His two children were forced to repeat classes over and over again. Ministry had become a vicious circle for him.

As soon as he heard the church in Ibadan was experiencing some challenges from the attendance because many of the members had left, he lobbied to be reinstated. Reluctantly, his superiors agreed with the condition that he had to build up the church in six months. Like flies flocking around dead meat, word went round that Pastor Yemi was back in Ibadan. All the old members rushed back. New ones came. Things began to happen again. When Pastor Yemi walked, his members walked. When he settled, his members settled. He saw it as a good sign.

One Sunday morning, the members flocked to the worship centre to pay obeisance to their God. Very few noticed the changes till Pastor Yemi drew their notice to it. The name of the church had been changed.

"We are moving to the next level" he said in his message. "There is something in a name that can make or mar a vision"

The G.O. sent police men from the head quarters with enough curses to destroy ten men. Yemi's members stood by him like the rock of Gibraltar! It was a strategic plot. The rent for the building was due and the headquarters had not renewed it. Yemi had paid for two years to secure the building under the name of the new church. The old church was fighting a lost battle. They withdrew their equipments but then Yemi had new ones on standby. He had been ready for a long time. The old church was suddenly non-existent. Staunch members left and sat at home while nursing their wounds but they were in a ridiculous minority. From there, things went from good to best. The church grew from strength to strength. They vacated the rented hall and built a magnificent building to the Lord.

Fulfilling several prophecies about his call, Pastor Yemi began travelling out of the country to honour preaching engagements. He had ordained several pastors who worked along with him. These men and women worked hard to move the ministry forward but soon it was apparent that the church wanted only their pastor. The more pastor Yemi travelled, the more the attendance in his church dwindled. When he was around, things went well, but when he wasn't, nothing happened.

When Pastor Yemi announced in church that God had asked him to relocate to the United States of America to begin another church, it was the nail that sealed the coffin on the ministry. Suddenly, their three-thousand seater auditorium was heaping cobwebs. Pastor Yemi had moved on, and so had his members!

————⊰⊱————

"I think the lesson here is that nemesis still catches on people, even pastors. The Tobiases must have resumed business full-scale" Paul said snugly. Bishop Jose laughed.

"You do like that don't you?" he smiled. "But that is not the reason why Pastor Yemi's church failed. Vengeance is mine says the Lord. We have to learn to let Him deal with all those issues. Yemi may have settled with God and the G.O. you know. That though doesn't mean he won't pay for wrongdoing. What I know is God takes care of that His own way. Now listen and this is strictly for pastors only. It wasn't the curses or the nemesis that ruined Yemi's years of labour. It was the modus operandi!" Bishop Jose sat forward and cleared his throat. "What many pastors don't know is that the scripture; 'there is that scatters and still increases, and there is that withholds more than is necessary and tends to poverty'; applies to more than financial and material gifts. If you build the ministry around yourself, what do you expect? When you're not there, nothing will happen. You need to empower people, and you need to train people. You need to scatter wisdom and knowledge and your contacts and experience amongst people who have the call in your congregation and among your workers. It is a good thing for you to travel and your members don't miss you too much; they don't miss the presence of God. You need to trust people. Don't be selfish with your platform; elevate people. The joy of the father is more in the success of his son than in his own. If Jesus had not called anybody to work with him closely, where do you think His ministry would be today?"

"But people disappoint you. People hurt you. Look at what Pastor Yemi himself did to his G.O!"

"But the G.O.'s ministry continued in other cities and I can assure you, he would have sent someone else to Ibadan. The point is that you cannot afford to go it alone and Yemi should have known that. The handwriting was on the wall. When he was transferred the first time, the church collapsed and almost folded up. Yemi thought it was because the people loved him. Huh huh, wrong wrong wrong. It was the first sign that he needed to do something about the people surrounding him. If your people love you, they'll show it, but it's not by replacing you with God. A pastor friend of mine joked about his members. He taught them to look to him as he looked to Jesus. Listen to me; you'd better leave it as a joke. The veil was torn. If you keep blocking the view of people from seeing Jesus, the day God decides to shift you, they'll also shift away. Some may be lost. I tell you now that ministry is not about you, it's about God. Your success is a failure if you do not have a successor."

"Hear hear, my Bishop" Paul nodded profusely.

WISDOM FOR PASTORS

MAINTAINING COURAGE

TUOYO LIFTED HIS BALLED fists and rubbed in soft punches into his shoulder blades. His well-toned arm muscles jerked in protest but he was too engrossed to notice. Suddenly Pastor Erebi's routine check into the lives of pastors and members in the monthly pastors' meeting was turning into an ordeal. It had started with a simple statement one of the pastors, Alaba, made when they switched from the issue of follow-up to welfare.

"Female pastors all over the world take welfare seriously" Alaba had said simply.

"And…" Tuoyo looked pointedly at Alaba.

"And our pastor should too" Alaba said.

"Is she an exception?" Tuoyo asked incredulously. He had joined Pastor Erebi's church after she preached at a lunch-hour fellowship he grudgingly attended at his office. He had never been one to take preferences to female pastors. In fact, until then, he believed women should be silent in church. But when she shared explicitly from the scriptures, he was bought. He continued to attend the lunch-hour fellowship regularly until he decided to visit the church on Sunday. After that he never looked back. He identified her as his prophet and though she was a mature, single woman, he had never had any problem submitting to her which in itself was a miracle. He loved and respected her and on more than one occasion, assumed a more prominent role in her life than the other pastors. Himself a mature single man, he had nursed the idea of having an intimate relationship with her several times. And though she was a little older, he had never seen it as an obstacle. Rather, he had not yet summoned enough courage to speak his mind to her. In the meanwhile, he appointed himself her guardian.

"If we want to go by what people are saying..."

"What are people saying?" he asked heatedly.

"Pastor Alaba, please continue" Erebi said, shutting Tuoyo up, mellifluously.

"It is not my opinion but I should be and I am interested in what people say in this church. I have heard people say that our pastor in insensitive to the needs of members which is unlike the nature of every woman"

"What else have you heard?" Erebi looked round the room. Pastor Alaba, the pastor in charge of welfare maintained a steady gaze. Pastor Nwanibe was taking jots furiously. He wasn't even the secretary of the house. He was Pastor Alaba's friend though, and pastor in charge of the youths and singles. Pastor Ruth in charge of the children's ministry shook her head when Erebi's gaze landed on her. Elder Nosa in charge of the Women and Men's Fellowships nodded as though in wonder. It was Pastor Temi, in charge of follow-up who spoke.

"We need to apply wisdom with all we have been hearing. Definitely, no doubt, there's been a lot of talk"

"When you say, a lot of talk, do you mean issues we should be concerned about?" Pastor Ebi in charge of music and sound looked at Pastor Temi, speaking with her shrill voice.

"If we don't have to be concerned, would it be brought up here?" Pastor Idong in charge of Hospitality and Protocol looked at her snappily. "Members are leaving the church everyday; do you think it's for picnic?" Pastor Ebi made to answer with a snide remark but Erebi's hand went up in the air. She cleared her throat before she spoke.

"Pastor Tuoyo?" her enquiry surprised everyone as Tuoyo seemed to be sulking. But when his gaze met hers, he melted. She looked lonely and in the midst of wolves.

"I want Pastor Alaba to please be plain. We want to know what you have been hearing and who has been saying them" he said stiffly. As Pastor in charge of outreaches, his position was just one more thing that drew him close to Erebi. Apart from the church treasurer, Pastor Angelo, and her secretary, Sister Esosa, no one else came close.

Pastor Alaba cleared his throat.

"Nobody brought me to this church" he started. I came by myself and I am convinced of why I am here. But I cannot shut my ears to the concerns of members. That's why I am here" he looked round. When he was sure he had all their attention he continued. Tuoyo stole a glance at Erebi and saw she was fighting for control. His heart went out to her.

"Let me make it clear that I have only the interest of the brethren at heart, and I believe that anyone standing in the way of the progress of the church should be addressed, regardless of who the person is". Tuoyo began to tap his feet quietly. His gaze remained subtly on his pastor. He saw the torture she was going through and hoped within him that this meeting would not change her. He had seen this kind of confrontation before in the church he was in before getting transferred out of town. The mess had scattered the church.

"When pastor begins to have sacred goats and cows and giving her time and preference to them alone, it is a problem. Our pastor must treat everyone equally. Otherwise, what are we doing here? Recently, I noticed that Pastor chooses the people she gives assignments to, for what? Are some more anointed than others? The other day, I was so ashamed when I walked into a meeting of some people and they were talking about our pastor having an affair with someone…"

"Permit me to interrupt you…" Tuoyo said heatedly.

"Permit me to finish" Pastor Alaba said heatedly. "If pastor wants to marry, it is not a sin! But if she wants to sneak around with men, it is not permissible"

"You are talking about an anointed servant of God!" Tuoyo stood up angrily, banging the conference table they sat round.

Pastor Alaba flew to his feet, shouting. "If you want to sleep with our pastor why don't you marry her first!" he snapped. A soft murmur went round the room. Tuoyo's mouth dropped. Erebi's face crumbled and for a moment, he thought she would burst into tears but when she spoke, her voice was strong.

"That's enough, both of you. Let God judge between you two, and if I be a servant of God, let the truth divide! This meeting is over till there can be sanity in our midst" she stood up, and walked out.

"Is it because she is a woman? A single woman?" Pastor Paul looked at Bishop Jose.

"You know the answer to that question" Bishop Jose said. "If you still don't know then you're ready for disaster in your ministry"

"It has nothing to do with gender"

"You're right. There are Achans in every ministry. There are Judases for every messiah, discover them and treat them with courage. Listen to me, when someone close to you starts sharing gossips with your members, you must stand on your feet and address the issue. You are a servant of God and your judgment is in His hands. You cannot afford to let anyone look down on you. Remember Paul and Timothy. Paul admonished

Timothy not to let anyone despise his youth. And that's what I have to say to every man with a call on his life…"

"And woman, Bishop"

"And woman! Very important. Do not allow anyone to despise the call of God on your life. If it hurts you so badly, go into your closet and weep in secret. And let your comfort be in the arms of God. They want to see you crumble or sometimes, they just want to be heard. Deal with them, wise as a serpent, harmless as a dove".

"You must be tired sir" Paul checked his wristwatch.

"I am but I was just about to hit on your curiosity"

"My curiosity sir?"

"You want to hear my story don't you? You itch to hear it" Bishop Jose looked at the younger man teasingly. "Or are you satisfied with the rumors you heard?"

"I refused to listen to any of it, sir" Paul said patriotically. It was true. He made sure he told off even his colleagues who feasted on the downfall of the great bishop.

"But you want to hear it now" Bishop Jose moaned and self-restraint. If he laughed now, the young man's intense look would soften. Instead he suffered with to maintain control.

"It's late sir, and I know you are tired. I won't want to push you. I mean, I've learnt a lot already…"

"It's alright young man" Bishop laughed. "Most times you don't see it coming…"

WHO THE PASTOR LOVES, HE PAMPERS

SOMEHOW, TRUTH WAS CREEPING up on me and I didn't even know it. I had started out in ministry like John the Baptist. Before ministry, I had been wayward. My parents had disowned me so many times it had become a joke in the family. I dropped out of university after two years and roamed the streets. Whenever my parents got fed up and threw me out, I took up any odd job and sustained myself till someone would talk the old folks into taking me back at home and I would have food and shelter again. Then I would carry women home, drink and get drunk, smoke, stay out late and one day, get everyone at home fed up till my father shouts 'ENOUGH' and I'm out. Then in the arms of a prostitute one day, a group came preaching and I got saved.

My conversion was so drastic it took so many months for my family to accept it. The first sign of a genuine change was that I went back to school. And in school, I became hooked and addicted to Jesus. I preached at every opportunity I had. I got so passionate for God that soon, it was inevitable that I start a ministry of some sort and so I did start a campus fellowship. I had never really been pastored by anyone before and suddenly, I had hundreds of students looking up to me, and I… I looked on to Jesus… for everything. When I graduated, I handed over the campus fellowship to my assistant and visited often. Then I got a job and continued with ministry. It was obvious I would lead a church. My passion for God burned so hot. I started the church with only three members but it grew to a whopping two hundred within the first year. I resigned from my job after then and got married to one of the most faithful sisters in church. I was so hot for God the only thing I considered when I decided to get married was passion for God. God blessed our marriage with three children in quick succession.

I had been so engrossed in ministry that I was never prepared for the victory that hit me. The church was large, the children were fine and money was easy to come by. I was becoming restless and did not know it. Restless and careless. I could have anything I wanted at anytime and unconsciously, I was taking this liberty for granted. I was becoming larger than life. Truth was poking me in the face and I wasn't sure why. All through the early days, I had pushed every other thing aside to face the work. All my life was about the work of God. Every other thing came second; wife, children, family and even myself. I guess I was becoming like David, strolling on his roof top at the time kings went to war. And that truth presented itself first, as a young man called Marvellous.

Brother Marvellous was every letter of his name personified. He was in every way marvellous. Immediately he joined the church from only heaven knew where, he became involved. He went through the beginners' class. Graduated top of his class and went to members' class. As class captain, he came top of the class and went into the stewards' training. He was captain here and did best and enrolled in the ministers' class. Within three years, Marvellous was a trainee minister in the church. He brought this new wave of motivational speaking and was an orator by no mean way. He worked in a soap factory as the control manager and never allowed his stiff schedules at work to jeopardise his work and commitment in church. He just won everyone's heart. In his spare time, Bro. Marvellous endeared himself to my family. My children loved him like a big brother. I saw him as a young man who was hungry for God. He was a talented instrumentalist and played best on the sax. He was a saint, only that everyone seemed to think he was not... after a while.

A sister reported to another sister who reported that Bro. Marvellous had been fondling her in the secrecy of his house. The truth came out when the sister started feeling guilty about it. When confronted, Marvellous denied it with venom; to the accuser's face. She only shook her head and feebly asked him why he was lying. The case died a natural death. After that, one or two complaints would get to me and when I asked Marvellous, he would query my trust in him. He would query my sensitivity as a man of God. Would God not expose him to me if he was a fake Christian? I reasoned with him. My wife was another story entirely by this time, and refused to involve herself with most things that bothered me so she had no opinion about Marvellous but the children loved him and he helped her to run errands. So she was happy with him.

Gradually, I noticed that the complaints reaching me about Marvellous had reduced. They finally died entirely. I saw it as a good sign. It meant Marvellous was actually right. He had been vindicated.

It was not true. He had won in quenching my sensitivity. He had stolen into my heart and locked up the strong man. He was a thief who had come to steal kill and destroy. And I never knew until he'd taken what he wanted and left. Marvellous proved as the first sign to me that I had become at ease in Zion. When he finally left, I could not even say the extent of the damage he had done to me. He had ruined me. He had awakened a dead man in me. I wonder why he did it. I wonder why he spoilt me so badly after all I had done to accept and love him. He must have been an apparition of the enemy. With Marvellous, I finally began to believe that demons could turn to humans to visit and destroy man.

———————◈———————

"What did he do to you, Bishop?" Paul stared at the tortured look on the face of the old man. Suddenly, he seemed older than his sixty-something years.

"Marvellous came to our church about twenty-five years ago, and the ruins of his deeds are still around me" Bishop Jose said huskily. Paul thought he wanted to cry.

"Should I get you some water?" he jumped to his feet.

"No, sit down. From the archives, the files always have lots of dust. As soon as we clean them, it will be alright" the Bishop narrowed his eyes for a moment and then smiled. Paul thought he was losing him. "Marvellous" and he heaved a heavy sigh.

"What did he do?"

WISDOM FOR PASTORS

LEVELS - BOYS TO MEN

A LOT OF THINGS I had never taken care of started becoming important after Marvellous became my personal assistant. I trusted him so much, I became like a child in his arms. I must say that looking back now, I can't blame him. He was thirteen years younger than me, had just gotten married and should be as such much less wise! Ministerially, he was my offspring. I had put several road blocks on the way to ensure that deceptive people and con-artists did not get into the pastoral team or even the minister's league but Marvellous jumped every hurdle. He was patient. He was smooth. He assured me he had what it took. He spoke in tongues more than all my pastors. He was also an orator. When he conducted service, church was sweeter than other times. I did not think it was necessary to pray about Marvellous before making him my personal assistant. Until then, I had none. He pointed out how much I needed one. And he was right. I was missing appointments, and forgetting a lot of things easily. I desperately needed an organiser. At the time he surfaced, I was being invited to huge meetings. All over the country, calls were coming in for me. My television ministry had taken on such a large audience that correspondence had become difficult.

"Daddy, you need help. I can't even believe that at your level, you don't have even a PA. I know men of God that are not half your size, boys, who ride hummers and employ MOPOL officers." Marvellous said passionately.

"Oh Marvellous" I laughed. "What is my size that you know those men of God are not even half?"

"Daddy, you are too humble. That's just my problem with you. See even Moses needed to relieve himself of responsibility at one point"

"So who would want to be my personal assistant?" I asked incredulously.

Marvellous laughed. "Who would not want to be? We can make announcement in church and interview people…"

"What about you? Are you not already doing much of what a PA would do?" I asked him.

"Me, Daddy! I'm a small boy o. In fact; the pastors would never accept me. There are even more senior people who joined the church before me… they will just start telling nasty stories about me again to spoil your mind…"

"Okay. You'll be my personal assistant"

Marvellous was a marvellous personal assistant. He watched my back like a hawk. He also kept me updated. Men of God are riding jeeps Daddy, when are you going to buy at least one. Your wristwatch is too simple at your level; people will think you are stingy to yourself. That handset is just ten thousand naira more expensive than what you want to buy but the status symbol is something else. On and on and on they went and I found myself conforming. He was so persuasive. Soon, I had a personal protocol department. Then I had a motorcade. The church could afford it anyway and I enjoyed the glamour. I was not hurting anyone anyway. The church building was done, the schools and the hospitals and the university were all making very good progress. I had churches all over the world. My name was rating high in the international scene and I was way under fifty years old. My strategy to win the world was working. I saw my vision of being a voice in the world coming to pass, and Marvellous was helping me achieve it. He was on top of the whole team. When my trips were too frequent and crowded, Marvellous graciously resigned from his place of work to work for me permanently. I was so grateful for his thoughtfulness; I doubled the salary he was earning. He insisted on only the best hotels and screened my preaching engagements to a select and choice few.

One day we were lounging at the Manor hotel in Kent, after a particularly successful meeting in London, when Marvellous looked at me with a troubled expression.

"Papa" he called. He had since changed from calling me 'Daddy' because 'Papa' was trendier. "Why won't you accept to become a bishop?"

I started to tell him it was ridiculous and unnecessary. To what end. It was just a title that meant nothing. Another status thing maybe but then for what? Almost all my friends were bishops anyway and it made little difference to me. I even had a friend who was an archbishop. So what?

"Papa, it's because you refused to see the significance of the title. So many people already call you bishop so it's not as if you are trying to use the title to make up for the anointing but there are some government quarters and occasions you'll not be allowed to function in because you're just a pastor" he snickered.

"Which one? At Aso Rock?" I laughed. I was a regular guest at the presidency already.

"At Aso Rock, Papa. Yes. What did this Bishop Emmanuel preach last time at the annual national thanksgiving service, nothing?! He just made some noise"

"Son, be careful" I said, controlling a chuckle. "Touch not my anointed o"

"I mean no disrespect" he said quickly and went quiet. It made me feel guilty that I had shut him up. He meant no harm.

"So what does it take to become a bishop anyway?" I asked lightly.

"Papa, I'll find out" he said enthusiastically.

Two months later, I became a bishop. To prove his point, I preached at a very important government occasion just about a month after my ordination.

"Levels have permanently changed, Papa" Marvellous whispered into my ears during the luncheon that followed the occasion.

"Sir, I don't want to sound naïve but…"

"Don't say anything just yet" Bishop Jose raised his hand.

WISDOM FOR PASTORS

IT'S A POLITICAL WORLD

IT DIDN'T SEEM SO at first but increasingly, it looked like a competition. My life had gradually become a roller coaster of events. When we hear about someone entering a city to do a crusade, we send a team to the same city to find out how far. Our team basically reports on what the other people did. We talk to the same local pastors and impress them more than our 'rivals'. Then we hit the city bigger and better. If the rival took four jeeps in, we take six. If they used the best hotel, we take two. It sounds unfair to refer to them as such but it was the trend! Gone were the days when we went into the needy mission fields alone. Like one of the pastors presented it, 'we need the money from the cities to reach out to the lack in the suburbs'. It was simple and plain. And we had big sponsors in most of the major towns and cities. Deep down in me, things did not sit right. I knew something was missing. I was an evangelist. I loved to win souls. I loved to feel the heart beat of God. I loved to pray long and hard. It was what made me tick. Even when my marriage began to fall apart, I took my solace in the presence of God. But I noticed it wasn't there anymore. And I just didn't know how to retrace my steps.

Suddenly I realised some of my pastors who had left the ministry might be the missing link. They were people who had worked hard to build up with me at the beginning, toiling alongside and most importantly, giving constructive directives. They were not there anymore. They had gone to start their own churches and I missed them. Desperately, sometimes. I felt selfish for not releasing them with my heart because I knew I needed them. Now I had Marvellous and a host of young people who were dynamic and knew nothing of the old time religion. They were fast-paced and believed fasting and prayer should be done by the prayer band alone.

One of these young men was called Joshua. Everyone however called him Man of Valour because of his dynamism. He was a power-preacher and had a very good command of the word of God. Despite their similarities, he never got along well with Marvellous. He could preach and teach with such fervour, I enjoyed taking him along with me to ministrations. While I sat and watched with pride, he would either, preach, teach or prophesy before I mounted the podium. I guess Marvellous saw him as a competition. But before I knew it, Joshua grew big under me. Though he had his flaws, they meant nothing to me. I encouraged him to take ministrations when they passed through me. But Joshua started going behind me to honour invitations. He made alliances with 'friends' and 'foes'. And this continued without my knowledge. Because of his charisma and attitude and spiritual altitude, I gave him more responsibilities than the other pastors. He stood in for me most times when I could not make an appointment. In essence, Joshua became second in command to me. Out of all my pastors, he was the least qualified. No matter what Marvellous had to say on this one, I stood my ground. Just as he was special to me, Joshua had found a mark.

I was relaxed and lounging at home one day when one of the pastors walked into the house. He was forlorn and looked ready to cry. He had been with the church for a few years, and though he wasn't so much a firebrand preacher, he was a soft-spoken and dependable teacher of the word. Besides, I could rely on him to be at meetings promptly. He was one of those slow-talking, slow-thinking people that would do anything for you. He was a treasure to the ministry.

"Pastor Fidelis" I greeted him as he stood and crouched against my feet, another ingenuity of Marvellous. 'Why would your pastors be greeting you, standing? Papa!'

"Papa" the middle-aged man greeted.

"Your soul is blessed" I said. He remained squatting as I sat down.

"Papa, I need to let you know this. I have a leading to leave the ministry"

"You do?" I asked dryly. He was a man I respected but he was also a fulltime minister. One of those ones I paid more for their loyalty than their productivity. How would he feed his family of one wife and six children? Where would he go? Who would take a paid pastor who could do nothing but be faithful to his overseer? He was ridiculous and pathetic.

"I have laboured in this vineyard, and it seems as if all my labour is in vain" he groaned.

"And?"

"Papa. Papa, I know God speaks to you but look at Joshua there. He…"

"Don't bother to make complaints about Joshua. You know you are nothing compared to him"

Fidelis' head dropped and he began to sob.

"Look at you. You are a sorry excuse for a pastor, and I encouraged you. I even gave you the pulpit a few times"

"Joshua has been manipulating you, Papa. He's plotting to even break away with half of the church" he looked at me pleadingly. His eyes begged me to hear him out. Mine hardened against his pleas.

I laughed out loud. "Joshua couldn't even break my church and take one tenth" I said sarcastically. I meant it too.

"You gave him all the top jobs. Favoured him more than those of us who have been with you since…"

"Favour is not fair. You of all people should know that" I said and stood up, dismissing him. He stood up also, and looked me straight in the face. He had never done that before.

"This is not favour, Bishop Jose" he said stiffly, sniffing back his tears, and anger.

"It is politics"

I began to walk back into my inner chambers and stopped short at the tone of his voice. "I agree with you. But then, we live in a political world" I snapped and stomped away.

Fidelis left the church. He was the last of those who believed in the old time religion. Joshua also left the church but I crippled his ministry so badly, he had to run back to me, after years of slaving and reaping nothing.

Suddenly, it seemed I had become more than a pastor. I was a Capone.

"Sir, what were Joshua flaws?"

"He didn't believe in a pastor praying and fasting. That was the work of intercessors. He used to dictate the amount of honorarium he wanted and in that at least, he and Marvellous agreed. And he used to negotiate. If the price was not right, he would not honour the invitation"

"Merchandising! My God!!"

"I stopped blaming them long ago, Paul. They had a pastor, didn't they?"

WISDOM FOR PASTORS

OCCUPATIONAL HAZARD

PASTORS WERE MEANT TO be protected all the time. That was my philosophy. We were servants of the most high God for crying out loud. No weapon formed or fashioned against us could prosper. God had given angels charge over us and that meant we didn't need external or physical protection. It had been a debate between Marvellous and I for long. He believed in bodyguards with dark-bones and black suits, and walkie-talkies, just like the president's men had. I believed in the invisible power of angels. We haggled over it several times. He wanted armed men in the protocol department; men trained to kill, sharp-shooters who were not necessarily born-again. When I ruled that out, he opted for the less regime-like type.

"We will interview people from the church and then send them for training" he suggested.

"Worse idea" I said. When he tried to argue, I shook my head and ended the story there. We didn't talk about it again for a long time.

I had a crusade in the city of Port Harcourt at the beginning of the year. It was in the peak of my ministry. I had my prayer team come in a week earlier and the planning committee three days before me. When we arrived at Port Harcourt, we were lodged in the Presidential Hotel. Immediately, I locked myself up and took time to pray and prepare myself.

I never felt comfortable with all that 'crap' about intercessors doing all the praying. It was meant to be a four-day programme and I was the main speaker, and it was an awesome outing! Even after being in ministry for over twenty years; I had never seen God move so absolutely. Every single person on wheel chairs stood up. Not one single blind person went back home in four days. The healing anointing was astounding. I saw people plagued with HIV stand up from stretchers. Each day was even better than the previous. It seemed as though God was doing something. As though He was making a gallant entry or departure, as the case may be, from my life and ministry. Families were healed from terminal diseases; people were saved by the thousands. Each new day, the crowd doubled till the stadium became too small to take us.

On the last day, I had two dead people on my hands. The first one was a young boy who had died just that morning. He had had an epileptic attack in front of his home and fallen into a ditch, hitting his head on concrete. It had a fatal impact on him. By the time they got to the hospital, he was brain-dead. He was just ten years old. The mother refused to give up. She had attended the meeting the previous day and seen almost-dead HIV victims stand up and stagger around a little before jumping and dancing and shouting. She took her son to the meeting grounds from the hospital and stayed there with him till evening when the meetings started. I took one look at her and told God to do what only He could do. The words had not left my mouth when the epileptic seizure got hold of the boy. He started foaming and rolling on the ground as though he had never been dead earlier. The mother and the whole crowd screamed for joy and fear. The boy was alive but sick. Members of the medical team rushed forward and administered first aid for his situation, bridging his mouth so he would not clamp his teeth. When the confusion calmed, the boy lay limp, weak on the floor at the altar. Weak but alive. His eyes were trying to roll back. I raised a chorus and the stadium went up in a roar, worshipping God and setting themselves up for a miracle.

Unknown to us there was a woman in the crowd. She had attended the meetings everyday but never thought God could intervene in her situation. Her middle-aged husband had been dead for over a month. He was the breadwinner of the family and had been in the mortuary all the while; his wife and family trying to raise money to bury him. At the meeting was also his first son, a sixteen year old boy. They nudged themselves and took a decision. It was time for God to bring their father back to life. They rushed to the mortuary and got the man out.

By the time they returned, the meeting was getting to a close. Several people had been healed and many more saved. The epileptic boy had suddenly jumped to his feet and started running round. It had opened the meeting in grand style. I was not in control any longer and I made no secret of it. Several times, I was broken myself and as people fell under the anointing, so did I. When we finally started to close the meeting, with every single person saved, healed, happy; there was a ruckus at the entrance of the stadium. This woman and her son brought in their frozen breadwinner!

I saw God doing something; proving something to me. He had started with a situation that scared me to death. I had never seen a dead person raised. And was planning to end it with an even more compelling scene. The woman was weeping and begging God to bring her husband back. Every where went silent when I began to sing. If God decided t do this, He would. If He decided not to do it, then nothing would make the man thaw. So I called on the Commander. Rain fire, O God, I screamed. Melt the ice! Bring back breath! Do what only you can do! I turned away from the corpse and knelt down, gripping the stand of the pulpit. People were singing along with the worship leader; the prayer band members blasted in tongues till sweat broke from their faces, as thick as blood. Suddenly, someone screamed. It was the wife of the dead. I continued to pray, refusing to be distracted. Someone shouted; it was one of my doctors.

"He's melting, Papa!"

I heard a cough, more screams and then shouts. I burst into tears.

The meeting finally ended at around midnight. I was worn out and yet couldn't sleep. I kept asking God, and myself, what just happened in Port Harcourt? I had been to Port Harcourt a million times. I had held power crusades since being a little child-in-the-Lord. I had visited other people's crusade and never in my life had I seen this kind of thing. As Marvellous helped to serve my meal; which I didn't have much appetite for anyway, he talked excitedly.

"We need to come back to Port, Papa. This was awesome. How did you do it? God! If we didn't have a church in this town already, we would have been foolish not to start one now! Chei chei! Papa, I fear you now o. Do you know how many calls I've received already from churches? In fact, we should raise the stakes. Two hundred and fifty k, if not, no ministration! God, Papa. I thank God for bringing me to you. Where would I have been if I'd listened to all those people with little foresight, who tried to discourage me from following you around? Hmn, Papa, it's you I'm following o. No one else. Now jealous people will be craning their necks to see what else we would do? They have not seen anything. Hmn. Eye has not seen, ear has not heard…Ohh…"

His voice droned on and on and I switched him off. Why was I not excited or elated? Why would God do such mighty deeds in my meeting? Why should this kind of good thing confuse me? The feelings within me raged.

"You know fame and pride are hazardous to spiritual health?" I asked softly.

"Ooh Papa. That's always my problem with you. You're always uptight about success. Anyway, I'll leave you to rest, and sleep. And maybe I should even send you a special gift to brighten you up a bit"

He left my room and went into his adjoining room.

A little after two in the morning, as I was just dozing off, I heard a light knock and the door opened. The room was pitch-black and for a moment I thought I was dreaming. But the cool body that touched mine under the sheets was nothing near the best fantasy you could have about a female body. I couldn't see but the feel was soft, fragrant; slim, yet full. Naked.

"Marvellous' gift?"

"Marvellous' gift"

Paul jumped to his feet and shoved his hands in his pocket. "How could he have done that? After such a meeting! What was he thinking?" he exclaimed and scratched his head. "Where was Mama? Oh my God!" strength left his limbs and he slouched into another seat.

WISDOM FOR PASTORS

CAREFUL, DON'T TRIP OVER!

THE LINE BETWEEN SANITY and insanity is invisible.

I had heard that it was thin before, but now I knew it was actually in your mind and when created, it was almost non-existent. When I woke up at mid-day the following day, I knew I had finally crossed the boundary. The day after the greatest crusade of my life and I wake up sinfully late wound up in the arms of a mermaid. She had not relented until almost sun-up! I stood up and put distance between us. She did not say a word; just a smug smile. It would have been ridiculous to shout at her to get out after saying all the things I'd said in the heat of the night. Things better forgotten. I decided to take the track of a fool. Cover the sin. Look normal. Be chivalrous! Preach.

"How old are you?" I turned to look at her from the safety of the window front. She sat up and failed woefully to conceal creamy nakedness with the bed cover. I thought it was intentional.

"Twenty-two" she cooed, smiling and gazing at me beneath long eyelashes and dreamy eyes.

"You shouldn't be here, do you know that? I could be your father" I said. She burst into laughter, throwing back her head, and flinging already tousled artificial hair about her face. More skin showed.

"I wasn't like a daughter a few hours ago" she teased softly.

It angered me. What was that scripture about the mighty falling? Of course I knew it. I had quoted it several times. But not today, please!

"Get dressed and leave" I turned to look out. My room overlooked a beautiful garden and the poolside. There were several people relaxing; ignorant totally of the hell I was in.

"I'm sorry. The crusade was very powerful" she added. The sheets rustled and I turned round, shocked, but just in time to see more nakedness as she stood up from the bed. Without the sheets! I swung back to face the pool.

"You were there" I muttered.

"I'm an usher in the church. You fulfilled my fantasy last night"

Suddenly I burst into laughter. Marvellous had arranged one of my own daughters-in-ministry to spoil me! "Is that supposed to be a compliment?" I snapped. I wanted to turn but remembered. "Cover yourself up" I barked.

"God will forgive us. He understands"

"Leave God out of this"

"Marvellous said you needed a woman. I thought I was helping"

"Get out!"

Somehow I was too ashamed to rebuke Marvellous. After all, you could force a horse to the river; you couldn't force him to drink. So I acted like nothing had happened. And he acted like nothing had happened. I was grouchy and touchy and though the rest of the team wondered why, Marvellous respected himself, and kept away from me. What gnawed at me the worst was the fact that I enjoyed that woman. I was glad I had her, from the safest confines of my heart; I was relieved to sleep with a woman after all I had been through. I was wayward and she was indulgent and that's the best way I could allow myself to reminisce what happened.

I couldn't rebuke Marvellous. I was guilty and though it was my secret, it was a secret. In fact, I indulged Marvellous to tend my wounds. It wasn't the first time I would cheat on my wife. Sometimes I even forgot I had a wife.

WISDOM FOR PASTORS

SHE'S EITHER A WITCH OR A WIFE

CALL HER MRS. JOSE. Or Lady Jose. Or Mama Jose. She was your typical Christian mother, with the arms and every other element that went with the title. I had married her when I was young and vibrant in ministry. She was a dynamo. Bose could do acrobats in the place of prayer anyway you want. She could fast for as long as you dictated, pray sing, preach and teach. When I met her, her spirit was more visible than her face. I loved her for everything she represented. And because I was so engrossed in the things of the spirit, I didn't notice she was plump. Neither did I notice her dirty-brown complexion or her natural hair. In fact, I never saw her until after we were married. And it was all my fault. In her own special way, she was beautiful. She had bright eyes and a very engaging smile. She was warm and homey and quiet, a truly submissive woman. Too submissive for my good.

The differences started showing even though I had been dissatisfied all along. In those days when we got married, it was sinful to question physical attraction. As long as we were spiritually compatible, God would settle the rest and that was that. When I started getting real physical attraction with other women, I thought I was backsliding. I knew I liked fair-complexioned women with slim-figured but shapely and well-endowed curves in the right places. But that was when I was in the world. A yellow girl would hunt me down any day, but dark women were a major turn-off. And here I was, married to one. I had the orientation in those days that God would not give you what you want, but what you need. I needed a good, homely and churchy wife. And that was exactly what I got. And I dared not complain about the dryness and deadness of our marriage bed. I married her as a virgin and there ended the good news. She was frigid and thought I was 'rotten' anytime I tried to teach her 'stuff'. And the basal needs refused to go away. I prayed and fasted; went for marriage seminars and asked the most obscene questions anonymously. Still I got no help. I didn't have a woman n my bed and though ministry grew and things went well, I was losing it.

The first time I cheated, was while she travelled with our children to visit her family. We had been married for seven years. We had three beautiful children. I was so pressed for a woman that day; I drove out, hoping to get air. I had not had sex with my wife for six months prior to that and the last time I touched her, she had cursed me. Who would I cry to? I was dying. So I rode around some main streets in town and on my way back, noticed a whore by the road side. She was just the type. I picked her up and took her to my house! I was too decent to have her in my bedroom; I took her to the guest room. I paid her heavily and sent her on her way early the following morning.

I was sure I had purged my desire for the next whore.

I was wrong.

Over the years, I hid my deadly habit very well. I even almost indulged my wife. I pretended I was loving Bose while in the arms of a harlot. Sometimes I would call her name in the throes of passion. Somehow, it vindicated me of any crime. And it also emboldened me. What happened to the Jims of America was happening to me and I was incapable of stopping it.

And concealing it.

I never got to know who the informant was but one beautiful day, as soon as I was finished with a lady in a secluded hide-away inn, I stepped out of the building to step into my car, I stepped in Bose's arms. She was with the children and Joshua. When I froze and opened my mouth to speak, she brought out a knife from her bag and slit her wrist. The whole place went into pandemonium.

Bose did not die that day. According to the doctors, the thick layer of fat under her skin saved her! But our marriage never remained the same after that. Two specific changes occurred. One, I detested her to the point of avoiding her; even in public. We started sleeping in separate rooms and I never allowed her to accompany me to meetings, occasions or socials again. We never had sex again! The only thing that bound my wife and me together was the roof covering our heads. I was offended that she had tried to kill herself in front of our children! Two, I became shrewd with my life. Not even Marvellous knew my movements. I was erratic and unpredictable, and precarious. And uncontrolled. Suddenly, I was leading a double life. In church, I was like a god. Afterwards, I became anything I wanted. What puzzled me was that God allowed me to go all wild. And still He used me. Before the visit from that usher girl in Port Harcourt, Marvellous never 'arranged' a woman for me. And not afterwards either.

Or so I thought. I would later discover he knew about everyone of them. Arranged most.

WISDOM FOR PASTORS

CAREFUL, CAREFUL DON'T TRIP OVER!

"MY LIFE WAS ON a downward trend and there seemed to be no stopping me. You see, I was a 'big' man of God" Bishop Jose shook his head. Paul was sobbing like a child and he did nothing to stop him. "Crying is good you know. I had a lot of time for it while I was in prison"

"In prison sir!"

"I spent a week in prison when one prostitute reported that I had raped her. She was going to make a lot of noise and she wanted revenge not money. Bose did not even know I went to prison. Joshua and Marvellous covered up well. They paid the police men to shut up first, and then paid the girl to allow me to be released and the charges dropped. They told the church I was away for a prayer and fasting retreat. I had never even seen the girl before"

"Joshua and Marvellous believed?"

"I don't know but Joshua had caught me in a sleazy hotel before. He was there the day Bose tried to kill herself"

"Your wife did not help matters either" Paul said, his shoulders slouching.

"I should never have married her you know. It was part of my fault. If you are not okay with a woman, don't marry her. You have a call on your head. Many men and women of God get destroyed because of the person they married. However, it was also my fault. I did not deal with the demons of my past. I had it in me to womanise and I just pushed it aside. You have to get proper healing and counselling, probably deliverance from your weaknesses. Some you need grace and a good partner too but where you find yourself married to the wrong man or woman, indulging in sin is not the solution"

"I'm afraid of marrying the wrong woman"

"Let God choose for you. We men think we married a witch when she starts acting up, it may not be true. She may just be reacting to the wrong environment she finds herself in. you can't handle it, she can't handle it. War breaks forth at home. God has a great choice if you'll just let Him. And it doesn't always have to do with spiritual strength"

Marvellous was married to a preserver. Despite all the fact that he was challenged with, she stood as a rock. She wasn't your typical pastor's wife. In fact, at one point in their relationship, she had dreadlocks on her head. But she stood stoically with him. A luxury I unfortunately did not have.

But it had not always been true for them. Marvellous first called her a witch before I did mine. She was slow and uninterested in church 'gra gra'. All the noise and excitement turned her off. Coincidentally, she was as much the opposite of Bose. And the two women never got along well. Bose expected her to be active, as his wife. She expected Matina, (that was her name) to do all the wifey things: be in church on time, act nice and good and be it. Matina was not it. But when the dam broke, she was his wall of strength. She was there throughout. I had never believed she could be so supportive. The witch was now the wife and the wife had turned to witch!

"After that great crusade, it just seemed as if the demons were resuscitated against you" Paul looked at him, heaving.

"I told you what happened on the night of the last day. Was that not enough to resuscitate demons?" Bishop Jose chuckled bitterly. "I personally resuscitated the demons when I returned to Port Harcourt the following week"

"What's your name?"

"Susana" she said, and smiled. "Interesting we didn't get to it the last time" she teased. A toll bell went off in my head and I shut it down.

"Don't you feel bad?" I asked as calmly as I could.

"When I'm with you, nothing matters" she squeezed her slim body against my back and I groaned, making her laugh satisfactorily.

"God matters, Susana"

"I like the way you call my name"

"You'll be surprised what a strong, young beautiful body could do to a man" Bishop Jose said softly and Paul turned on him.

"What is the meaning of that sir!" he said between his teeth. "Do you know what your downfall did to thousands of believers? Getting caught in the arms of a child your daughter's age? You can even reminisce and miss it!" Paul shouted at the elder.

"What is truth is truth" Jose whispered. "When you're fallen, there's no where else shame can take you to"

"But you mustn't stay down, must you?" Paul banged his hand on the stool beside his seat and groaned. The tears were beginning to trickle down his face unaided. "We watched you suffer in the public and ached for you and yet you're not even sorry" Paul snapped at him.

"Not sorry" Jose smiled. "You don't know what happened do you?"

"I will pay you to understand" Paul turned on him.

"Well, listen very carefully then. And listen to me when I tell you that your anger with me is justified. Listen to me when I tell you that dignity compelled me to go into hiding. After the whole thing blew into my face, no one needed to tell me to go away. That's why I left church and everything else. I left the country. That way, I don't get to pollute anything or anyone"

"True saying that the higher you go, the greater your fall"

"The greater the risk, of a fall, Paul.

Who could have expected I would end the way I did? Not me. My marriage was over. All that remained of it was a façade. But I had gotten through that and continued to pretend everything was alright. I had lack of nothing; not money, not women, not fame. I could sit down and ask for, anything, and I would get it. So when Joshua broke away, it made me sit up. It was a Herculean task but he managed to win about a thousand people away to start his ministry. That was less than a fifth of the membership at the headquarter parish. It did not hurt me in the least but that Joshua had stabbed me in the back. A couple of my closest aides advised me on what to do, and I did it, and it worked. Six months after breaking away, Joshua was seeing the fruit of my seed. His church did not last much longer and he came back to me. He pleaded that I accept him back and I did.

I did not know that Joshua had discovered I was the cause of his misfortune. What I did was not fair. It was outrightly mean. Joshua had been like a son of my body and I knew all his weaknesses. He was an unforgiving man. And unknown to me, as I plotted his downfall, I also plotted mine. Because when he found out I was behind his problem, he never forgave until I was ruined. And he stopped at nothing to see it happen.

I planted criminals in Joshua's church, under the disguise of converts. They came into church, faked a salvation experience, and plundered the church. They stole from the account severally, raped the sisters in church, and conned the brothers. On several occasions, they came to church on Sunday morning and staged a real robbery, beating people, taking their money and injuring people who struggled. One such bloody attack almost ended the life of one of Joshua's pastors. Gradually, people left the church.

Then the criminals entered Joshua's home and one of them lured his wife into a relationship. It was the toughest of the challenges but they pulled it off. The young man was handsome and charismatic. He did not pretend to be close to Joshua. In fact, Joshua hated him. Somehow, he got into Joshua's bed. He had slept with Joshua's wife several times, winning her confidence and love before he staged a display. He wanted Joshua to catch him in bed with his wife. And it happened. Joshua was so outraged that he tried to kill the man but, ur, a criminal? The young man beat Joshua black and blue and left the house. Joshua could not take it. He sent his wife away, and taking the advice of his friends, thinking it was the curse I placed on him working, returned to my church. I thought I had taught Joshua a good lesson.

"Bishop"

"Paul" Bishop Jose groaned. "Joshua took his time. He carefully plotted everything and systematically uprooted every secret I have ever had. The climax was when he brought Susana to the church convention to make an open confession"

"He is the one?" Paul gasped.

"He is the one" Jose said gruffly.

"We only heard that a reliable source close to you brought everything out. And Mama added her own facts to the confession"

"That wasn't hard. She had had it with me. And I never blamed her"

When Paul looked at the Bishop's face, there were tears... a silent waterfall. Pain welled up inside him like a woken giant and he burst out into loud pain-filled sobs.

"Oh how art the mighty fallen, and the weapon of war perished" he screamed.

WISDOM FOR PASTORS

EPILOGUE

A GOOD WORD OF wisdom for pastors is from the African proverb that says, DO NOT LOOK WHERE YOU FELL, BUT WHERE YOU SLIPPED. The work of the ministry is not the work of the flesh. And the Bible says we have a HIGH call. That is not easy. The work of a pastor is more complicated than any other profession. You are man and spirit. As a man, you are expected to be perfect. As a spirit, you are expected to do the impossible... always. Allowing the flesh to rule is courting with disaster. There has never been a two-way about it. Once decisions are taken to satisfy the basal needs of eating, drinking and making merry, without first and due consideration for the preference of God, there is bound to be trouble.

God is not unfair and He is not unjust. He is not unruly either. He gives you opportunity to excel, to stand up, to prevail. He gives allowance for weakness and steps in with His strength. But only if you allow Him. Deep down, you know what is right. Just do it. Please do it.

Your mistakes go a long way. They are not ordinary mistakes. They are the mistakes of a shepherd. If the shepherd is smitten, the sheep will surely scatter. They are the mistakes of a head. If the head is cut off, the body cannot function. Take heed to the ministry that has been committed into your hands and see that you fulfil it. Guard your heart with all diligence for out of it flow the issues of life. Trust in the Lord with all your heart and lean not on your own understanding. In all your ways acknowledge Him and He shall direct your path. Remember; Wisdom is found on the lips of him who has understanding. May God strengthen your hands to do the work He has committed into your hands. Amen.

WISDOM for PASTORS' WIVES
Lu 7:35 "But wisdom is justified by all her children."

Dedicated to my sister:
Adetoun Fadugba
… who birthed me, spiritually.

CONTENTS

DRESS WELL, WOMAN: YOU ARE THE PASTOR'S WIFE!

WHEN BHEKISISA OPENED THE letter, the first thing that caught her attention was the emboldened heading: Dress well, woman: You are the pastor's wife! She hissed first and then called her husband's attention.

"Who wrote the letter?" her pastor husband, Lungile asked.

"Anonymous" she said, looking at the bottom of the typewritten letter.

"Throw it away, then" Lungile said lazily, looking at the Bible in his hand intently. He had been in his study, reading the Bible, praying, meditating and preparing for a ministration he had later in the week when Bhekisisa breezed in with the letter.

"With this kind of heading?" she sneered. She didn't exactly know how she felt.

"Well then, read it and throw it away" he sighed, sparing her a glance for a brief second. Bhekisisa started reading quietly and then exclaimed. "What?" Lungile closed the Bible and looked at her.

"Listen to this: 'I have watched you closely ever since I knew you and to my dismay,

seen a downward trend in your way and manner of life especially dressing. What do you want the women committed into your hands to think? The scripture says you are a role model, a city set on a hill that cannot be hid. When you start wearing skimpy things like that small black dress you wore to church last Sunday, you will cause havoc and send many sisters to hell…' This person was in church last Sunday" she said, alarmed.

"He's someone who's been studying you and waiting for a time you'll miss it. Get rid of the letter" Lungile said and flipped a page of his Bible.

"How are you sure it's a he?" Bhekisisa asked. She suddenly realized her heart was beating harder. No, she thought. Not someone familiar, close.

"The man obviously has a crush on you" Lungile said lightly, and Bhekisisa hissed.

"Oh honey, you make such a slight issue out of this. How will I cope with people criticizing me, watching me…?"

"Come on, people watch you all the time. You are the wife of a pastor. Every member wants to look at you"

"I don't know what to do or think. I won't wear that dress again. I…"

"I like that dress on you. It's not all that short anyway, knee-length is acceptable"

"Even though" Bhekisisa looked back at the letter and finished it off, shaking her head.

"Let me read that" Lungile said, setting his Bible aside and giving the attention he now realized she needed. He read through the letter carefully and looked at her beautiful face. "You know this letter is not fair. You are not the woman described in this place" he said, waving the letter in her face.

"Obviously this person does not think so. They don't approve of me" Bhekisisa whispered and covered her face.

"Don't be ridiculous, dear" Lungile threw the letter on the table and pulled her into his arms. She wasn't an ugly woman; 'desperately seeking for ways to be more beautiful' neither was she 'trying to conceal the inner ugliness with an outward beauty'! As the letter referred. How cruel could people get? After pastoring in the church for ten years, it still baffled Lungile that Bhekisisa struggled with his members over matters he considered trivial. At some point when they couldn't have children, Bhekisisa had been bitterly criticized to be barren, by the members. When their set of twins finally came close to eight years after they began pastoring, everyone who had something to say had swerved to attributing their breakthrough to Lungile's purity and spirituality. Now trouble-hungry members were seeking to destabilize and make her unhappy. The previous week, a female elder had softly criticized her for wearing light make-up. Two meetings after that soft reproof, she had not seen her new make-up kit eye-to-eye. Much to Lungile's disapproval. If you try to please everybody, you'll kill yourself, he'd told her and that was just the previous week.

You can't please everybody because within the brotherhood, there are contenders and accusers of brethren, working for their master the devil, amongst the ranks. As a pastor's wife, it is wisdom to listen to as many as are willing to talk to you. Listen carefully and objectively, sieve the truth from the chaff and prayerfully make adjustments. It is not godly neither is it classy for a pastor's wife to be rigid, stiff and unapproachable. There's nothing cool about it. Rather, you repel your husband's ministry and teach otherwise with your life. On the other hand, you can't afford to be tossed to and fro by every 'Sarah, Jane and Judith' or 'Tom, Dick and Harry' who has an opinion to share about the pastor's wife. Study your congregation; note what acceptable conduct amongst your own world is. Then adjust and abide by the rules. You are their first assistant shepherd; don't let the food you feed them with nauseate them. There are many pastors and visions and manifestations amongst brethren, share them, feel them and practice them. Be relevant to your parishioners so much so as to catalogue every change and every phase. Let your people see you as a caring mother but one who firmly knows and holds her own. It does not affect your spirituality negatively.

I WANT PASTOR, NOT YOU!

THE FIRST TIME IT happened, Efe thought it was a mistake. She sat through the counseling and ignored the darting eyes of the couple as they spilled out issues that were affecting their marriage. It wasn't until they left that Nosa addressed her concerning them, politely implying she stay away the next time. But she had had good suggestions to make and the couple had been grateful she sat in on the conversation. And so she had continued to sit in on counseling sessions with her husband. Most people coming for counseling wanted pastor but none ever confronted her, the way she had it the day Alero came in.

Alero was a senior business lady who first started worshipping with the small congregation Nosa and Efe pastored. Up till when she started with them, their financial status had been epileptic. The numerical strength of the church veered between the fifties and the sixties, many of them women, children and students. It was one of the students who brought her aunt, Alero to church. Alero had been having serious marital issues. Her first fiancé duped her of over five hundred thousand naira of money she planned to invest in her rice and oil business. When she got herself out of the disappointment of that whole ordeal, ready to love again, she met Tuoyo. Within a few months of meeting they set a marriage date. On the set date, Tuoyo was nowhere to be found. Alero later discovered he had run off with another, much younger lady. For a lady of Alero's financial and physical maturity, fast clocking thirty-five, she became desperate and fell for Luke; a renowned dupe. Alero claimed she loved him badly and would do anything to keep him; and Nene was given the option of paying the bride pride. Privately, Alero arranged the amount from her business confines and sent to Luke's family in the village to bring to her people. She never saw him or his family after that. Still Alero ascribed her ill luck to nothing. She moved on with her life and later met Ehis. He was the real smooth talker and loving beyond reason but Alero was four years older than him. He didn't mind really but his mother would have none of it and up till their wedding day, his parents and family rejected her. It was her mother who advised her not to show up at the wedding venue. Her little cousin, who was a member of Nosa's church felt so troubled about the trend and took Alero to her church.

After attending the church for a few times, Alero decided to seek counseling with Pastor Nosa. Unfortunately, someone had tipped her off on Efe. On the day of the appointment, she arrived late and missed Nosa. He had gone out of the office to see someone else. After exchanging pleasantries, Efe invited Alero into the small, sparsely furnished office she shared with her husband.

"You can talk to me" Efe said softly. Nosa had hinted her of Alero's appointment and problem. She had a particular soft spot for successful, single women.

"It's okay, ma. I'll wait for pastor" Alero said.

"I don't know when he'll be back but he told me you'll come so why wait when we can share your problem together" Efe tried to encourage her. "Do you think it is a spiritual manipulation?"

"What? Oh, Mama, please" Alero laughed uncomfortably.

"You can tell me, really" Efe smiled.

"I told Pastor about it and he said we will pray together" Alero said. "I want Pastor to pray for me himself" she said as politely as the statement could sound. Efe felt as though she had been dealt a slap. She wanted to say 'is pastor's prayer stronger than my own?' or 'do you think God answers his prayer more than mine?' Then she got infuriated with the 'old maid' and wanted to lash out with something like 'I pray for pastor who prays for you, who's more potent? Me or pastor?' or even, 'I woke pastor up to pray this morning after spending a full hour in God's presence. He prayed for only five minutes'. Instead she sighed and smiled stiffly.

"I'll excuse you then"

One of the things that a pastor's wife must come to terms with is her position in the ministry. Especially if she's not a preacher herself. Many people see the preacher, the one with the word, the one with revelations and prophecies. They trust their pastor more times than they trust their pastor's wife. There are exceptions of course. If you are not one of the exceptions, don't take it hard. It comes with the territory. One of the best ways to cope is to overcome the feeling of inferiority to your husband is to engage in things you really enjoy and are called to do. If you are the praying type, face it squarely; if you are a singer, dancer, usher, actress… whatever one, magnify the office. If you are a counselor, prayerfully help those who come to you. Trying to make a point that you are as competent as your pastor-husband may just yield the opposite result. Remain where you are and allow God to work through you to affect people's lives for the better. When you understand this, and patiently practice it, you will be fulfilled and able to act freely and easily with your members, without giving your husband or members the feeling that you are competing with their beloved pastor.

WISDOM FOR PASTORS' WIVES

YOU ARE NOT A GOOD PASTOR'S WIFE

ALICE WAS ONE OF those women who never bargained to marry a pastor. She had met her husband when he was in the Navy. She could never forget that experience all her life because it was so unique. A man in well-starched white navy uniform had slowed down his brand new black Peugeot 307, on the road as she tried to get a taxi from Gwagwalada junction into Abuja main and asked if he could give her a lift. She had declined politely. She wasn't the sort that took lifts from strangers. He drove off at once and she sighed. A few minutes later, he came back and stopped in front of her, again, she declined and to her amazement, the weather changed. It was the most unusual rain she had ever experienced. It was February and the harmattan season was having its fun day. No one envisaged rain on such a day and people scuttled around in desperate need of shelter. Alice had longingly gazed after the free ride speeding away, regretting her decision. To her amazement, the driver began to reverse. This time he simply pushed the passenger's seat door open and she promptly entered. The first words he muttered almost shocked the life out of her.

"I'm sorry, I asked God for the rain so you'll be forced to take the ride. Forgive me. I'm Lt. Col. Ofianya Ochima I'm from Benue State"

"You asked God for the rain?" she asked incredulously, ignoring his polite manners.

"Yes. I have driven past you about eight times now. The first few times, I didn't have the liver to stop and ask you to take a ride with me" he said simply, concentrating on the road.

"Do you know me from somewhere?" she looked at him as though trying to figure the face out.

"No o" he shrugged. His heart was actually beating very fast. He had never stopped to give a stranger a ride before. But he was a prophet of God, and God had given him a word, concerning her.

"Do you just stop and give strange women free rides?"

"God forbid. And you are not a strange woman. Where are you from?" he asked. He navigated smoothly towards the unity grounds and sailed towards Garki, where she was actually headed.

"Why?" she paused. "Well, Benue too. I'm from Ukor but my family lives in Otukpo"

"Thank God then. It's a confirmation"

"What's a confirmation?"

"You'll one day be my wife!" he had admitted bluntly, refusing to look at her. She had remained mute not just because she lacked words or thought he was insane, but also to floor him. He would never know what was on her mind. When he stopped in front of the estate her aunt lived in and turned to look at her, she was dazzled and a terrible fear gripped her heart. He was a dashing man with a picture-perfect face, soft and yet angular-hard. His unusual features enthralled her and for a moment she thought she was in the same car with an angel.

Eight years later, married with three children and a happy settled home, Ofianya had called her with quiet confidence and told her he was convinced he should leave the navy and join the ministry full time. From there, it had been a roller-coaster ride with God. They pastored with several ministries and before God, Alice tried to adjust to the life of ministry. She was used to navy calls but her mindset about ministry was totally different. Ofianya had been a medical doctor while in the navy and he used his knowledge as part of his ministry to humanity.

One bright, sunny day, a member of the church flashed her several times. The man was one of their members who had a flare for calling on the pastor at a moment's notice, making demands. He was also one of those people Alice tired of and showed. Being the person she was she hardly could hide her feelings about the overbearing man. Between them, the message remained clear, stay away from me. On this particular day, though surprised the man was 'flashing', she ignored the call. Ofianya was praying at the time and had asked not to be disturbed. Alice threw her phone aside, telling herself she didn't even have credit to call anyway. When her husband finished praying, in his characteristic manner of sharing his experiences with God, with her, asked for the said man.

"He was flashing me but I didn't have credit to call back" she explained.

"When?" Ofianya asked calmly.

"Let's see" she opened her handset and checked. "About three hours ago"

"His daughter should have died by now" he said and picked his car keys.

"What…?" Alice tried to follow him as he headed for the door.

"Why didn't you call back?" he barked at her, angrily. "Why didn't you alert me?"

"How was I to know his daughter was about to die? Why didn't you go when you knew?" she ran after him, upset he was trying to lay the blame on her.

"Because" he stopped so abruptly, he bumped into her. "I also had a peace that you would act as promptly as I would" he said before he slammed out of the house. His heart beat rapidly as he left. Please God, spare that child for me. Please.

On many occasions, you are tempted to feel like a failure. A situation comes up, at times, it is a matter of life and death, and you are just not sensitive enough to take action. It doesn't mean you are a bad person or that you are a bad pastor's wife. All it means is that you need to be more yielding and attuned to your husband's ministry. Many times, you are encumbered and stressed out. It takes an extra duty to be a pastor's wife and when you were not fully prepared to tackle that responsibility, there is the tendency to fall short. Sometimes it is so glaring that it is the members that bring your shortfall to your notice or your husband's. They make it look like you are incompetent, sometimes useless. Even people prepared to enter ministry with their husbands face such challenges. Here's my advice:

• Change your orientation about the ministry. It is as much your responsibility as it is your husband's.

• Pray for God to make you more sensitive to the needs of your husband and the flock in your care.

• See yourself as able to perform and help; complement your husband in ministry.

• Move on and learn from your mistakes. Don't go around having pity-parties and crying over spilt milk. Opportunities abound in ministry, take advantage and fulfill it. Be a kingdom asset and not a stumbling block.

May God strengthen your hand to this good work in Jesus' name. Amen.

THAT'S WHAT OUR PASTOR DID FOR US

FREKKY BREATHED IN AND out several times, trying to control her raging emotions. She thought she was going to burst as Mrs. Ata Akpan continued to give her testimony. Several times, her face flamed up till she thought she would catch fire, but she stood calmly beside her husband and retained the pasted smile, she was so sure that if this did not stop soon, the smile would start to disfigure her face, because it was weighing down so heavily on her muscles.

"We also want to say thank you, once again to our dear pastor. If not for him, were will we be today. Last week just as the devil was dying of jealousy, our pastor brought to our house a bundle of goodies. There was nothing that was not in that parcel. Even up to clothes for the children and myself and my husband…"

"We thank God. We thank the Lord" Ukeme said from the pulpit and began to clap. "Halleluyah!" he laughed and the whole church rose in exhilaration, clapping and rejoicing with the lady. Frekky smiled more and joined in the clapping. Now she was sure her face would burst. How could she? How could they? All of them. She had given as much, if not more to the success of the 2,000-member congregation…

"We will now dedicate the first set of triplets in this church" Ukeme said breathlessly. Frekky moved forward with the first of the three and Ukeme dedicated him. Then, the second, a girl and the third, another girl. The service finished on the high note and church dispersed. Ukeme, as was his custom, waited back in his office for a few hours while Frekky went home with the children. Later in the evening, after supper Frekky called her husband into their bedroom. "I know I sound very vain saying this but please, I don't see how I can take any of this anymore" she started. Ukeme remained quiet, listening. "Today, that Mrs. Akpan went on and on and on and on about how wonderful you are and all and never once made mention of my part. I don't understand. When she went into labour, I was there, even before then, throughout that her pregnancy. I know, and we both know how I suffered with her. Several times I cooked with my own money for her. When she went into labour I slept with her in the hospital. I prayed with her. Fasted for her. And throughout the seven days she stayed in the hospital, I cooked for her and her whole family. Is it that she could not even say a simple thank you? She spent over five minutes extolling your wonders and not even a word for me!" Frekky said, her heart beat fast, hurt. Ukeme continued to stare at her. "Are you not going to say anything?" she asked. "Have you finished?" he asked dryly. She knew that tone but ignored it and sighed. "Well, there are a lot more to say but it's the way most people react to me. How many people appreciate me the way they appreciate you? It is so unfair. I'm not even saying they should give me things but at least a simple thank you" she looked at him. He continued to stare. "I have finished" "What do you want me to do about this?" he asked. "What sort of question is that?" Frekky asked tartly. "I don't ask people to appreciate me when they do. Do you expect me to start asking them to appreciate you?" "Well, no. It's alright. I'm sorry I brought this up. But if you appreciate me in front of them, they will learn to appreciate me" she turned away from him and began to undress, signifying she was through with the conversation. "Are you trying to blame me for Mrs. Akpan's oversight?" he bit out to her back. "You can be the judge of that" "Are you trying to annoy me tonight, Ndifreke?" he only called her full name when he was upset. She turned to look at him. She didn't mean to upset or annoy him and with his question, she began to really question why she had brought the issue up. It wasn't the first time she would feel so offended. Probably that was why the bottled-up anger was spilling out so.

"No" she said, clutching her cotton nightgown to her body. "It just hurts, that's all" she said softly. Her response softened him.

"I'm sorry, dear but I don't know what I can do to it" he shrugged. "What would you do?" he asked. She pulled on her nightgown and shrugged.

"I don't know" she got back into the bed beside him. "I'll probably point out that it was my wife that did most of those things" she shrugged again. She didn't feel right teaching him what to do. He ought to know.

"That's true. I'm sorry"

Two lessons to be learnt here.

1. Learn to speak out when you are upset about something. Even something as personal as appreciation.

2. Pass across your hurt or offence in an objective way, and to the appropriate person. Facing the offender may boomerang. Better face your husband in the secret confines of your bedroom at a time he can hear you.

It does not mean your every need will be met or that you will be attended to but it helps to relieve the pain. Most people see their pastor first, and foremost. Some see only their pastor. You cannot blame them, neither can you blame him. And you should not take it personally either. He would most likely receive more gifts and praises than you, he is the pastor. Some people mean it to spite you; some innocently overlook it and really mean no harm. It is not for you to decide or conclude on who means well and who doesn't. The point here is for you to maintain your posture even when things don't seem to be the way you expect. Keep your head up, and smile for your people. I love you for it.

MY FATHER-IN-THE-LORD, THE PASTOR

NJEH GIGGLED UNCOMFORTABLY AND looked at her fingers. No, they can't mean what they are saying, she thought. WHAT?! But she maintained her outward profile, only giggling once in a while. She thanked God Abua couldn't make this evening's programme. What! She exclaimed in her mind. She looked back up and listened as calmly as she could. They were in the annual PFN Pastors' and Wives' Forum and a pastor's wife had raised another 'funny' question in the marriage segment. The guest minister, a seasoned marriage counsellor, was answering a most embarrassing question about sex and the pastors were laughing and teasing their wives. Oh God! What sort of teaching is this? Njeh thought.

"Sir, I have to disagree with that view sir. I stand to be corrected" a pastor's wife stood up and everyone laughed again.

"What do you disagree about? It is not even a mere personal view, it is a fact" the guest minister said.

"Sir Sunday is a holy day. Pastors need to be in the spirit when they wake up, not thinking of…of" she sat down embarrassed, and laughed, pinching her husband.

"Let's survey then. I will start with your husband" the guest minister said. There was uproar of laughter. Njeh shifted uncomfortably in her seat.

Definitely, no one would agree with this man of God. "Pastor Sir, what do you think about making love to your wife on a Sunday morning?" he asked. The pastor stood up and shyly nodded. People tried to maintain a serious look on their faces.

"It is a good idea, sir" he mumbled and everyone laughed.

"What's a good idea?" his wife blurted out and reared more laughter. Njeh shook her head in shock at the pastor's response. Abua would never agree to this.

"It is a very good idea, sir. I think our wives should learn!" an outspoken pastor stood up and made some noise.

"Paradigm shift" another one shouted. The men started talking together, excitedly.

Njeh could not believe what she was seeing and hearing. Are these not men of God, fathers-in-the-Lord? Were these the same men who preach holiness and purity on their pulpits? The guest minister began to clap and the others joined in till the clapping ended and there was some sanity restored.

"You see one thing you have to understand is that sex is good. Sex is good for pastors too. They are human beings, men. Flesh and blood. And if you do good things before you leave the house for the day, only good things can come out of it. It is only because we see pastor's job as a spiritual service and sex as a carnal service; and thereby think that if we perform the carnal service before going out to perform the spiritual service, we will carnalise the spiritual service. You are wrong. Let me ask this: is there anyone here who has had sex on a Sunday morning, before church?" A few hands went up. "And you are supposed to preach in church that day?" Some of the hands came down, leaving only a couple. All were men, except for a woman, whose hand remained up, steadfastly.

"How come your wives did not raise their hands?" the guest minister teased. "Or didn't they partake in the action?" the wives of the two pastors raising their hands hid their faces, embarrassed. "Raise your hands, let's know what you've been doing" the man of God further teased. People laughed. The women raised their hands shyly. "You should always support your husbands, readily" he chided softly. "So who wants to talk about it?" he asked, shocking everyone. The wives quickly put down their hands but the pastor's wife who'd raised her hand all along started waving it.

"Even better. Let's hear what a woman like you has to say" he turned to focus on the woman. "Where's your husband?"

"He had to leave town just this morning. He is unavoidably absent, sir. I just want to encourage all our pastors and their wives to make love everyday, especially Sunday. It's like tonic" she said. The men burst in a loud roar of handclap, some even stood up for her. Others shouted 'tell them'. Njeh shook her head tenaciously. The guest minister noticed and looked at her as the lady took her seat.

"You don't agree?" he asked her.

"I'm sorry, sir. I had no plans to talk but I must at this time. Sex is not a chat-room topic and we must not drag the name of the Lord into it. I know I sound archaic but if my husband were to be here, he would have walked out of here. Sex on a Sunday morning is nothing but trouble. Please I beg us all to be sober. On Sunday morning, you wait on the Lord to hear from God, not... not..."

"I disagree entirely" the previous lady stood up, shaking her head.

"Alright I will settle this quarrel. Since I am still in town and today is Saturday, I want to give us all an assignment. Tomorrow morning Sunday, give it a try" the guest minister said. Njeh sat down shaking her head despondently. 'How are the mighty fallen' she moaned within. "And if you don't like it, don't ever try it again. BUT try, and be open. And if it works, if you like it, give me a call"

Abua returned home shortly after Njeh returned full of news of his journey. He kept quiet as Njeh gave him fillers on how carnal pastors had become. These were people who supposed to be spiritual fathers and mentors, high on the spirit on Sunday morning. He listened quietly, smiling and shaking his head intermittently. The following morning, Njeh had an urge to do the assignment. She struggled with the thought, casting the demons of carnality from her mind but then she told herself, if it doesn't work, 'I'll never try it again'. Especially since she didn't even believe a woman should make the first move. And so they made love in the early hours of Sunday morning before church, for the very first time in their twelve years of marriage and ministry.

That morning, not only did Njeh have the fun time of her life in bed with her husband, Abua preached with spirit in church. It was the first time in church that Njeh would see her husband so passionate about the message. Numerous people trooped out to give their lives to God. Several more needed to rededicate theirs and did. Abua preached on Remember God while there's time!

A word is enough for the wise. Go ahead, try it!

WISDOM FOR PASTORS' WIVES

WHO'S GOT YOUR TONGUE TIED?

TANDRA SAT MUTE, BURNING hot and cold in indignation. What exactly was going on here? Were her words no longer safe in the ears of her confidants? Had they become like bad seeds falling on bad ground and spreading evil in the midst of the brethren? Who would ever believe her if she tried to vindicate herself. To cap it all up, her words had been misquoted and of course, misjudged. Can't I cry for a moment, she wanted to yell but held her breath? She would allow them to finish. Her grouch should not be against any of them. Her grouch was against Rana. Rana was her confidant, her friend. The only person she could confide in. and now everything was coming out. Every minute, outrageous and compelling detail. She had not spoken to gossip or chat. Her words had been in desperation for her brother. She had only sought advice and a shoulder to cry on.

Andrian her pastor husband was too busy to listen to petty concerns, and she had no reason to blame him. Besides, there were several 'girly' things that bothered her and she couldn't bring herself to confide in even her husband. And there are just times when you need to unwind and talk to someone. Frustrations, advice, just someone to talk with…

"So we just want to know why you should say such horrible things about a sister, your member" Sister Ethel said, concluding the long list of accusations.

"I am sorry" Tandra said. "I meant no harm; I just needed to confide my fears to someone…"

"What fears, Mama?" Rasoherina said her voice shook with anger. Tandra almost jumped up to slap her. What insolence? All because of her brother? She blamed no one but Rana who had been talking carelessly.

It had all started when Zanahary her brother told her of his intentions to marry Rasie as they all fondly called her. Tandra's initial fear and concern had been for Zanahary. He was a quiet, unassuming and easily manipulated fellow and she had great fear about his choice of a marriage partner. When he introduced Rasie, her first impression was that the lady was probably older and too outgoing. She spoke rapidly and hardly allowed Zanahary's voice to be heard. Tandra expressed her fears to Andrian who dismissed them. Zanahary was past the age of consent. He was sure the younger man could take care of himself. Then Tandra heard a few things about her prospective sister-in-law; she had two children from a previous marriage she had run away from without a proper divorce; being the most incriminating fact against the bride-to-be, amongst other character flaws. Tandra was livid. She tried to speak with Zanahary who was adamant. Then she poured her heart to her friend Rana.

It actually wasn't her first time of confiding in Rana, but she knew it would be the last. Previously, Rana had blown her cover on minor issues but this time, it had become a serious problem. It now seemed as though she was spreading evil tales about another sister in church! And she was the pastor's wife!! That was thoroughly unforgivable. To crown it all, the story had spread round the church and she, pastor's wife is now summoned by some of the married women Rasie reported her to.

"Don't crucify me. I meant no harm. I have to protect my brother, is all" Tandra stood up abruptly. She vowed to kill Rana… then just decided never to tell her problem to a single soul on earth... again. She would rather die silent than stand the risk of this kind of humiliation.

One of the many travails of a pastor's wife is having a confidant, someone you can pour your grievances on. Even the Bible says we should 'confess our faults one to another, and pray, one for another, that we may be healed'. There is a necessity for every human being to have a confidant. As a pastor's wife, people want to know what makes you tick, especially because you are married to an 'anointed man of God'. They want to know how, if your husband fights with you; how he behaves when he makes love to you! And so many other things that are 'definitely none of their businesses'. Just being close to the pastor's wife and having first hand information about what was what is enough for some. They get close, get the information and boast of 'how pastor said and pastor's wife told me bla bla bla'.

It hurts when you need a friend and all you get are people who backstab and take advantage of you. Many times, you need an adult audience, someone who can help you sort through your thoughts. Yes.

Here's what I did, after getting battered a few times.

• I did not give up on finding a confidant.

• I forgave those who had let me down and just learnt my lesson not to share sensitive issues with them.

• I confide different sensitive issues to different neutral people, for instance, issues that concern my family, I confide to a non-biased friend; issues about my marriage, I confide in a young friend who's a pastor's daughter; issues about the church I confide in a friend of the church who's not a member, and so on.

• I confide in people who have confided in me. We share our secrets and prayers in secret.

• Other people's secrets I confide in NO ONE!

May God help you, o mother-in-Israel.

WISDOM FOR PASTORS' WIVES

LIVING IN HIS SHADOW

SERWA GAZED OUT AT the rain falling pelting on the roof of the house opposite theirs. It was a magnificent bungalow with a paved compound and a well-manicured garden. The fence of the compound was so high one could only get a view of the house from Serwa's house, in the sitting room of the two bedroom flat on the third floor opposite the road. Serwa often absent-mindedly gazed out at the compound that held her bound. The scenic view held her breath. Especially when the children came out to play, Serwa longed to have that fulfilment and peace. Now as she gazed sightlessly at the house, her sorrow rose up within her, again. Today, Adofo sat beside her and calculated away. It was end of the financial month and he was putting his books together for the end of month reports. The keys of the calculator being punched began to rise above the noise of rain and directly in Serwa's grey matter. Her head started pounding and she thought she would be sick. She wished the noise would go away. The rain, the calculator keys and her heart pounding so loud she thought it would burst.

"I'll go and rest for a while" she said to Adofo who simply nodded.

She walked into the strait, cramped room they used and dropped on the three and a half by six-spring bed. Virtually everything in this room was a gift. Serwa was very grateful for everything but she had often thought of living in real comfort, like people she reckoned to be her mate lived. But ministry had thwarted her dreams in many ways. She heaved herself up on her elbows and gazed at the enclosing walls of the room. She deserved better than this, she thought, and not the material wealth. She was not happy with her life. When she married Adofo, he was already a pastor in the mission he worked with. Their church was a Pentecostal church that had branches all over the world. The church president and founder was a man tremendously used by God and respected by man. At the time, Serwa was in the prayer band and also an executive in the youth fellowship. Going by preparedness for ministry, she was most appropriate for her husband. She understood his call and loved the ministry he aligned himself with. Shortly after they got married, Adofo who had previously been an assistant was given a pulpit of his own. They pastored in the church for close to three years before they were transferred to another state where they started a new church and worked there for five years. The church grew in their hands from nothing to close to a thousand. They were later transferred two more times before being sent to their present location. Though Adofo had grown in the ranks over the years, it had not added up to him in benefits. They still had to collect salary advance to pay their four children's school fees. The accommodation provided for their rank was small and inadequate. To top her misery, the policy of the mission did not allow the pastor's wife to have a paid employment so that whenever there was need for the pastor to move, the family could also move. Ever since they got to their new location, Serwa had grown weary of her life. After leaving university, and bagging a first class degree in banking and finance, se had met several of her schoolmates who were not half as intelligent as she was, doing well and fulfilling destiny. Instead, she found herself doing things according to the dictates of the mission and not even knowing what she could do. She had been unable to continue in her prayer band because of the outlined activities of the pastor's wife, along with her responsibility as a wife and mother. When she had insisted on attending prayer band night vigils on every Friday night, she had been rebuked for neglecting the women's fellowship meeting by eight in the morning of every Saturday. And when she thought she was not at all good for the children's ministry, she had been mandated to head it, because she was the pastor's wife. Over the years, Serwa withdrew and did her duty mechanically. She could not fit into the ministry she had been dumped in and could not find fulfilment; secular and ministerial. Gradually, she elapsed into depression. Her husband noticed all her struggles and tried to help. But on the other hand all he could assure her was to hold on. 'When we reach the top, you'll have more freedom to fulfil your vision' he said. After eighteen years and working in almost ten different churches within the ministry, Serwa was still waiting for that day to come!

Why sit we here till we die? The four lepers that asked that question got tired of their misery and did something about it. I like to advise every pastor's wife to have a vision and to have a project. You may not have the power to change policies if you are serving under another man's vision and no doubt, you may be limited. Even if your husband is the founder, you may still be limited but prayerfully find what you can do within the confines of your situation. If you have to lead the women probably because you have to, and not because you have a calling to, you can get for yourself an assistant who has the calling and allow her to fulfil her ministry while you lead. In leadership training, we are made to understand that a leader must not be a manager. If you don't have the call, be the leader and find a manager who does. It is also good to have a project. I have a very deep bias for welfare projects. Get involved in something you know you can effectively do to move the work of God forward. In that, you have an advantage as the pastor's wife.

WISDOM FOR PASTORS' WIVES

IT'S THE WOMAN HE MARRIED!

PASTOR BOLA OJO WAS a very charismatic one. He was your typical mix of choleric and phlegmatic. On the one hand he excelled and moved people. On the other hand, he was a very quiet and unassuming person. The phleg part of him was stubbornly determined while the choleric side bulldozed every obstacle. He was a rare combination of a man, with a fine blend of spiritual, administrative and personal. Everything he laid his hands on to do prospered literally. His marriage, as other things in his life, worked just as he liked it. He wasn't the overbearing type and often openly appreciated his wife in front of everyone. Tosin Ojo on the other hand, was an outspoken woman. When you analyze her, she was 80% of sanguine and 20% of everything else. Most often, she just loved to exhibit only her sanguine. She was the women's leader and pastor of the teens' church and she preached in church almost as often as her husband. In fact, aside her husband, there was no other pastor in the church. A couple of deacons worked with them to do altar duties but none preached.

Quarterly they held a meeting with the church workers and that particular quarter, Tosin had a lot of issues to tackle. She was upset with the ushering team for not being smart enough, two choristers were advised to step aside because they were caught fornicating, one of the deacons was suspended on her recommendation for beating up his wife and generally, everyone seemed to be messing up. While refreshments were being served, there was an unusual lull. Two sisters, one an usher, Dupe and the other a chorister, Yemi, sat together and brooded.

"This kind of meeting today, Pastor is really in a very bad mood and very unhappy about everything" Yemi said.

"I'm just as upset. See how Mama just washed all the ushers down after we did all our best. We have been complaining about the way people treat ushers and there you go, no appreciation" Dupe said sulkily. The meat pie she held in her hand tasted like sawdust.

"My concern is Pastor's reaction. See how he just kept quiet and just took everything in"

"Of course, he would not counter Mama in front of us" Dupe said. "I wonder who told her about Bro. Supo and Toyin sleeping together"

"Hm. You don't know anything. She'll go about smiling at us, making us feel comfortable around her. That's how she gets all the information she needs about people. Talk about green snakes"

"I'm surprised o. I used to love her so much" Dupe said.

"It's what happens when the man keeps quiet all the time. She's there raving and ranting and Pastor just keeps quiet for her, allowing her to make all the trouble she has the capacity for" Yemi shrugged.

"It's so sad o. As kind and wonderful as Pastor is. The woman you marry is important o"

"Especially if you are a Pastor with a call on your life" Yemi said.

"I think part of the problem is that Mama didn't expect the church will grow so fast. You know, obviously she can't handle the level of success they have" Dupe shrugged.

"Na wa o. Power has entered her head. I pray she will not destroy our pastor for us o" Yemi bit into the meat pie she'd been served. "Hah, this meat pie is tasteless. Where did they buy it from?"

"Mama arranged for it to be bought. You know she does all the buying in this church" Dupe said tartly and hissed.

Seated at the end of the row behind the two sisters was Mayowa, one of the younger members of the church. She listened with awe and displeasure and wondered how the sweet-looking, sweet-speaking and justice-loving pastor's wife could be so trampled upon especially by two people she had seen show the Mama overwhelming love and loyalty.

As a woman, you should be prepared to take all the blame for your wrong and your husbands; from family members, friends, your children, in-law and life in general. The woman seems to be the brickbat. As a pastor's wife, you are no different. You even have one more group of people who will blame you for all their problems, and that's your flock. If your husband is stiff and unapproachable, they say it's your fault. If he is too loud and outspoken, they'll say you made him so. It comes with the territory. Occupational hazard, they call it. Sometimes you get to hear it, sometimes you don't. It does not matter. What matters is how you handle it. Search your conscience and do what you seem is fit and best. Sometimes you may lose credibility and approval, it's okay as long as you are in God's will. You win some, you lose some. BUT! Don't take advantage of your members. Don't win some lose some till you lose all. You are their role model. They want to see you and admire you and love you. It comes in only one way: LOVE THEM AS CHRIST LOVED YOU. JOHN 13:34 AND 35.

WISDOM FOR PASTORS' WIVES

YOU MARRIED HIM COS...

WHEN LOLO GAVE HER life to Christ, she aspired to marry a pastor. It was her dream day and night and she was vocal about it. Whenever she had to talk about her aspiration, she delved into it excitedly and with conviction. Pastors were modest. They were dedicated and would never cheat. Pastors would love the Lord and minister to people. They would affect people for good and lead people into an eternity of peace, joy and love. With a pastor, she would have safety and protection from outsiders. Her life would be safe and secure, and people would love her. She loved being around people, loved respect and being respected. Everything she had seen in her own pastor's life held enthrallment for her. Her vision in life was to be a pastor's wife. While on campus, she was dedicated to God, more than most other sisters in the fellowship and it was no surprise to anyone that she became the Mama of the Fellowship and there Lolo received her first glimpse into a life in ministry. It helped to ginger her desire to work harder for God so her heart's desire would be met. She saw a wee bit of everything she had imagined life would be like. She mothered the sisters in the fellowship and in her time, the sisters' fellowship grew stronger. She was responsible also for the care of everyone in the fellowship, most especially the executive members. Lolo took delight in cooking for each member of the executive at least once a week and everyday for the president and the vice president.

She loved practicing what she had fervently prayed to God to be her life calling.

Shortly after her youth service, back in Portharcourt and working for an oil servicing company, Lolo met Nengi, a dashing, young minister. He was her dream come true. Nengi had just finished from the university and having a call of God on his life gone to a Bible College. There, he was seasoned and dried and prepared for life in a collar. He was posted to a branch of the ministry where he served as the assistant pastor, and there he met Lolo. She was your typical pastor's wife material. Though she worked, she was more committed than most. Nengi fell for her for more reasons than one. A year after there marriage, two wonderful things happened to them. They were blessed with a bouncing baby boy, and Nengi was given a parish to head.

Because of his charisma and hard work, success was swift. From fifty members, they grew to over a thousand in three years. Lolo's dream was coming true in full bloom but success for them was also like the rose bush. The sweet smell and the beauty drew you close but if you are not careful, the thorn pricks were very painful. Nengi's success fast got into his head. Before Lolo's very eyes, all the traits she had attributed to unbelievers began to unfold before her. Suddenly, Nengi became lavish with money, making demands from the church as well as from members. His lifestyle became extravagant and he made demands on her to the point that he openly opposed her way of dressing. He even warned the young ladies in the church at one point not to 'look like Mama'. Lolo tried to keep her calm; all she worked for suddenly seemed to be crumbling before her eyes. Her members gradually started disrespecting her, as they grew fonder of their celebrity pastor. Lolo started suspecting Nengi was having an affair but she couldn't make herself believe that. It would be too much heartache.

They had been heading the church for eight years and the congregation had grown to over three thousand. They had built their own property and everything was just fine. Lolo had started to settle down to the new life she now had. Her expectations of life in the ministry had dimmed enough to accommodate reality. Her husband had broken every code of conduct she set for a man of God. He had taken greedily from the church funds to satisfy his own selfish wants; he had slept with several women in and outside church and had abused her physically when she complained.

She had started living another life and never expected anything would take her by surprise. But on that fateful Sunday morning, she sat on her seat in church, facing her husband's faithfuls; they had since switched off her, completely, joining her husband to call her 'old school', she got the shock of her life. Nengi, after preaching a passionate message announced that he had resigned from the mission. Lolo almost slid off her seat in disbelief. To further assault her, he announced that the church building and name had been changed. Right there in front of everyone, he was taking over the property and mission of another. Would the overseer of their ministry stand by and watch this happen? People started clapping and shouting in jubilation. Some even went as far as coming out to hug and congratulate him. Lolo slumped on her seat.

What can you do when things turn this way? Please don't even let it. Understand first, that God has made you the sole custodian of your husband. Don't let him grow bigger than you. Oh not bigger in the sense that you are competing with his success but bigger in the sense of what you can handle. Learn early to have a mentor, a counsellor who he admires and respects. Grow with him as his success increases; don't be intimidated. You are his helpmeet. His guardian angel. Do your job. Forget about all the talk about his being a man of God. To you he is a man with flesh and blood. God did not make his flesh communion bread! Please, take care of your husband. Pray for him. Watch over him, look good for him, dress well and be clean for him. Don't assume he can take care of himself. Take care of him. Except he is a son of perdition, you have no problem. If he slips by and falls into error; face the problem like a battle. You are sincere. You loved him and married him. You love God, let God fight your battle and save your husband for you. Most of all, I feel you and may God help you because his failure and fall is yours too and more.

DADDY DOESN'T LIVE HERE... ANYMORE

PASTOR ANELE SAT AND stared into space as family members from both sides milled around the house, speaking in muffled tones. The children played out in the garden, perhaps oblivious of what was going on, perhaps not. Lungile and two of the other pastors in the church sat over the accounts of the church and looked through it, making plans, suggesting changes. Plans and changes. Those two words had suddenly become the most dreaded words in Anele's life in the past eight weeks. When the news came of her husband, Pastor Kanelo's death, breath had literally been squeezed out of her being. Where would she start from? That question had ringed in her head like the church bell, loud and sudden. Everyone told her not to worry, all is well. But she of all people knew all was not well. Kanelo had not known he would die. Till the very last minute, he had said he had a future. A hope. Now there was none. Because he was gone.

Mandy, their three year old ran in bare-footed, gurgling and sweating.

"Mommy, Mommy" she jumped on Anele's laps as Mercy, one of the sisters in church rushed in after her to take her away.

"It's alright, Sister Mercy. She can stay" Anele said, her eyes pleading

"I want Daddy" Mandy shouted, halting every movement in the room.

Anele's mother and elder sisters, three of them, turned from packing leftover meals from the funeral reception away, and gasped. The funeral which just took place that morning had been delayed because so many people had been involved and wanted to attend. Kanelo had been loved by everyone, the world over. Kanelo's younger sister cussed loudly from where she sat with a friend. His parents had been seated quietly in one corner of the room, and now his mother burst into tears, wailing actually. Pastor Lungile stood up abruptly, anger and pain made his body writhe. He clenched his fists as though to stop them from hitting out at the innocent child.

"Take her away from here" he blurted.

"No. I want her to stay. She doesn't know anything" Anele murmured. Mandy burst into tears at the anger, pain and misery her innocent words brought and Anele hugged her.

"It's okay, my dear. Daddy doesn't live here" Anele's mother came closer and patted the child's back.

"Daddy did live here. But he doesn't anymore" Anele said, with words she hoped to sooth the child. But those words had ceased to soothe her.

"Let me take her" Mercy said quietly and carried the tot back to the garden.

"You can relax now" Anele looked at Lungile who still stood, fuming.

"You know we can't. You haven't told her or the others of their father's... death. You refused to allow them attend the funeral. You left the church to roast; you're so secretive about everything. Your eldest daughter will soon be ten. She must know. They must know. You can't take decisions alone and you must..."

"Lungile, Pastor Lungile, please" Kanelo's father said stiffly.

"One must come to terms with these things" his mother said, sniffing. "It hurts badly but she must"

"Please excuse me" Anele stood up, and rushed out of the room.

"See what you have done" Lungile hissed. "She won't come and settle down to look at the books"

"It's too soon, give her time" one of the other pastors said.

"She'll never have time if you carry on like this" Anele's mother spat, following her daughter out with the other sisters.

"The church has been thrown into confusion. The members are disoriented. Pastor Kanelo left no plans, no will, nothing" Lungile looked round the room, tears pooling in his eyes. "We have worked too hard, to see this work go down the drain just because the visionary is gone. The vision is still alive. The 5000-seater auditorium is complete. The hospital is almost complete. The orphanage" he locked his gaze with Kanelo's parents'. They both looked ashamed, upset. "We have to run with it. Since this calamity, almost everyone has asked, who's next. People want to move on…"

"Kanelo was just forty years old!" his mother exclaimed. "How can you fault him for not having a will?"

"I don't fault him. I respected him. I still do. He accomplished what many of us could not even at fifty. I'm forty-nine!" Lungile argued. "You know, Pastor Anele never supported his starting a church. Never accepted any of us. He had always dragged her along. Now she insists he wanted her to take over from him. I am frustrated!"

Oh Pastor's wife and helpmeet. The love of his life, his strength, his supporter. I feel you. In all the pain, don't be alone. Don't be afraid. This is the time for you to draw in every strength, every resource. This is the time to look inwards and do the right thing. You do want to keep his vision alive. You want to carry on his name. You want to be happy! He's gone and there nothing you can do about it, except to live the way he would have loved to see you live. If when he was alive, he wanted you to be more involved in his vision, now's the time to do it. If he wanted other pastors or members or board members to be more involved, now's the time to work on getting it done. Occupy yourself with what you know would have given him pleasure. BUT only if it will give you peace and joy. He's gone!

He's joined the saints triumphant. He's joined the great cloud of witnesses and somewhere there, he's cheering you on. Don't clamp up, frustrate yourself and the people who loved and believed in him. Deep down in your heart, do you want to take over? Do it! Deep down in your heart, do you want to entrust the responsibilities to another pastor, someone you trust, someone faithful, someone the people love, someone God has spoken to you about? Go ahead. Don't allow fables and speeches of mere men; advice that are not inspired by God, to derail you. Trust in the Lord and in Him find your comfort. Hold on, hang on, and be strong. Move on! You are loved.

CAREFUL, DON'T TRIP OVER

AJEH MET WITH AGANTEM in a quiet corner of Lamoni Munchies. It was late and the restaurant was about to close. They had chosen the time specially to have some privacy. The large restaurant hall, now nearly deserted except for three women taking pepper soup and chatting listlessly at the other end of the room, was decorated in cool yellow and lemon tones. It added to the homeliness of the environment and the reason why Ajeh had chosen this location. Besides, the place was relatively new and she doubted she would bump into anyone she knew. The reason for the choice of the location had been Agantem's. He wanted as much privacy as she could arrange and she'd almost died of curiosity.

"Would you eat anything?" he asked nervously. She shook her head.

"A drink would be fine" she added. She studied him as he ordered a bottle of maltina for her and soda water for him. He had a strong, angular face, high cheekbones and stiff straight nose. His beautiful-shaped mouth was sheltered by a thin moustache. His clean-shaven face looked more beautiful than handsome despite its muscular features. He was a delight to look at.

"I don't want to waste your time, Mama" he said softly as soon the waitress left. "I asked to see you for two reasons both boiling down to the same reason. I need advice." He looked at the soft, cotton yellow and green checked tablecloth. She tried not to prompt him. "I think I can trust you?" It was rhetoric but she nodded all the same. He was reluctant and she was inquisitive. She wondered why he didn't seek her husband out. He was not only the pastor; he was a man like him but then there were some things that probably only a woman could help. Not if it had to do with Agantem's beautiful and sophisticated wife, Ayang.

"I'm…" he paused as he saw the waitress approach with their order. He nodded quietly in acknowledgment. Ajeh smiled at the girl before she left quietly.

"Yes?" she was forced to prompt him finally when he remained quiet, and slowly sipped his soda water.

"I'm having an affair with a woman…" he eased. Ajeh swallowed, trying to keep her calm. Let him finish.

"A woman in church. I know I should stop it immediately" he rushed on and then lapsed into another minute of silence. "It's been on for about five months now, and well, I guess I should be grateful I want out now…" he looked into her eyes for the first time, searching for a reaction. He was a well-respected man in church. He had a beautiful family, a beauty-queen wife, two lovely sons and a daughter all in their early teens. He was a successful research officer with the tourism bureau. An unfaltering member and steward in the church. He was in the logistics department. Why? How? Ajeh thought warily.

"You are wondering how that could be?" he half-smiled, the corner of his left side upturned. The expression made him look so boyish for a man in his early forties. "It started when I arranged that tour to the ranch for church members…" he sighed. "Really, I don't want to talk about that. I said I had two things to ask your advice about. The first is how I can start loving my wife again" he took a long gulp of his drink. "She doesn't know of course, but I think she suspects. I have been very discreet so I won't hurt her. She's been…" he struggled briefly for words. "I've found her so boring lately" he stammered the words out. She's adding weight in tons" he laughed but the bitterness behind his words warped the laughter and made it sound like a snicker. "We don't seem to have anything in common any more" he shrugged and finished his drink. She sipped hers slowly, studying him, asking God for advice, what to say.

"Did you talk to her about your feelings?" she asked.

"We haven't had a sensible conversation in two years. All you see in church is 'playing house'" he sighed as though he'd been relieved of a heavy weight.

"You have to find a way to talk..."

"I've tried several times, she ends up throwing tantrum which annoys me and sends me farther away from her"

"It's a sin not to love your wife. It's like breaking the commandment of God in Ephesians 5 and also like helping the devil" she thought it perfectly in place to give him a little sermon, a reminder of what he ought to know. "The devil wants you two to be unhappy and he's using you two to accomplish that feat. You have to fight him. Fight it" she said.

"I understand" he said quietly, unsatisfied. She pressed it.

"Adultery is abomination before God" she tried not to sound gentle, indulging.

"I know all that too. I guess I need to work harder on everything"

"You are the man, you have to make things work" she exhaled noisily. He turned his glass round and round. "You said you had two things to say"

"Yeah" he blew into the empty glass. "Please don't condemn me for this" he looked at her again with that deep look that was full of guilt.

"You can confide in me" she felt it was necessary to say it.

"Thank you. I..." "I intend to break up with that other woman this week but my problem is that I am having a crush on another woman right now..." she started to shake her head. "It's what's made me get over this other one. I need help to shake the feeling off. I need to stay away from other women who are not my wife" he shook his head.

"You do need that and desperately too"

"I never had a woman problem. I've been married for fifteen years, never once cheated on my wife!"

"It's the enemy coming in. you have relaxed and taken things for granted. Does this other woman know you want to call it off?" she asked.

"Yes. I hinted her told her there was someone else. She was upset" he gushed. Upset! Ajeh wondered how callous women could be, knowing this man had a wife in the house.

"It still boils down to one thing. It is wrong in the sight of God and immoral in the sight of man. Either way, you are in the wrong. This may be none of my business but who are these women?" she asked.

"Hilda Marshal" he said.

"What?" Ajeh gasped, unable to believe what she was hearing. Hilda was one of the most responsible spinsters in the church. Just the previous week, Ajeh asked her to lead the spinsters' fellowship. She respectfully declined and she'd wondered why.

"The person I'm having a crush on will interest you more" he said with gravity. His eyes disclosed nothing. She held her breath. She was sure the reply would hurt her and disappoint her more than the first. And she wished she hadn't asked.

"You" he said quietly.

Before Ajeh could find the right words, she stood up angrily. Agantem's eyes lit up in alarm.

"What is the meaning of that?" she barked and stomped out of the restaurant; thank God she came in her car. She fumbled with the locks and slammed out of the premises, hissing and hissing.

The following Sunday in church coincidentally, Ajeh took the message. She preached the message that had suddenly begun to burn in her heart over the past few days. The conflict between sin and madness. She told the church the whole story of how a married man could be messing around. She said everything, short of mentioning names. It later brewed hell fire in Agantem's home.

Or else, how could I have gotten to know about it.

----------●❈●----------

Tripping over is one of the dangers of ministerial duties. There's always that tendency of tripping in so many ways as a pastor's wife. First, you have privileged information; don't misuse it. Many people would normally not come and meet you for any advice if you were not their pastor's wife. That sounds hard but the earlier you accept it, the better for you. Privileged information should remain classified. It's not part of your preaching material, please. If you must use classified information on the pulpit coat it so heavily the owner of the story would think you are talking about someone else. Make it vague. Or make it a testimony that people can learn from and try your best to cut out the ugly parts. Preferably, leave well alone. If you must share stories, share those about yourself and if they are too embarrassing for you, then preach the word. There are enough analogies for you in the gospels. Second, you are a public figure and if you are finer than me as I guess you are; you are bound to attract a lot of people. You are the star for many people; help them to organize their emotions. Don't play on the emotions of your men and don't taunt them about it. You are a mother, play the role. Direct, instruct, rebuke, pamper. A fine blend of these will help you and your flock. Third, don't try to be a hero. You don't have all the answers. The one you can't handle, tell someone else who can. Fine, they may hold you in high esteem and trust you with all their problems, if you can't don't turn yourself into 'god'. There's nothing wrong with a statement like 'I can't help you right now but let me go and pray and think about this and I'll get back to you' or 'I can't help you with this one but let me ask someone who can; I promise I won't give away your name'.

The integrity of your office is paramount.

WISDOM FOR PASTORS' WIVES

MAMA'S WEIGHT

WHEN GABRIEL HEARD THE comment, his heart was grieved. Was it that someone needed a connection even in church to get things done? He had applied for the scholarship through the proper process only to be told a few days earlier that the scholarship had all been given.

"How? I thought they would call us for interview or something" he moaned to his friend and roommate Joel, who was also a member of the church. It had been announced about a month earlier in church that the annual scholarships were out and those eligible were to apply. Gabriel applied and was qualified by all means. He was a widow's son, had good grades in his entrance examinations, had an admission and could not afford the education. The church scholarship seemed to be his only hope. Besides, his mother was an executive member in the widows' and single mothers' fellowship. He was a member of the choir.

"Did you apply through Mama's office or you just went directly?" Joel asked.

"I dropped my application with the church administrator like they announced in church" Gabriel replied.

"Oh! You should have told me. Chei!" Joel exclaimed. "I thought you knew. It's in Mama's hand now. Ooh!" Joel hissed. He knew Gabriel really needed that scholarship.

"But they announced in church that we should drop our applications with the church administrator" Gabriel insisted.

"I was in church now. I know that entire announcement. It's just so that it won't look as if it is not open. Those applications don't even leave the church admin's table. Hm"

"How do I go about it now?"

"Maybe if your mother can go and see Mama, maybe but I doubt. Last year, my cousin applied and his mother had to go through Mama's secretary. Even at that, it was so hard. That's how I got to know that the entire announcement means nothing" Joel heaved a sigh in pity for his friend.

The building project was dragging and Pius was beginning to get weary. He had used up all his energy and tactics to raise funds from every avenue possible. His members were stressed and some had even started questioning his motives for taking up what they called an 'elephant project'. Pius had thought the headquarter church would pull in their weight when he showed them the vision for his parish but had been stunned when the senior pastor patted him on the back and told him 'well done'. Nothing had come from it after that. His motives, contrary to what the Samballats and the antagonists had said were very noble. He was single-eyed about the project. Now he was stuck in the middle. Contractors were cussing and fussing; he owed over five hundred thousand there. The Aluminum man was asking for his balance of twenty-five thousand for frames he had made but not fixed. The rent for the building they were using was due and landlord was spitting fire; in fact senior pastor must never hear of that because the money had been given him from headquarters. He had used it all to pay the advance for roofing.

Pius was mooning in his office, brooding and moaning intermittently when Seth walked in. Seth was the pastor of a sister parish in the same mission. After exchanging pleasantries he noticed his colleague's demeanor and inquired.

"The building project is choking me. I haven't touched my salary for the past six months and I've sold almost everything, my TV, DVD player even some personal items. I have raised money every way I can. I've reached here" he drew a sharp line across his throat with his right hand.

"Any help from above?" Seth, who still used a rented hall for his parish, asked in a relaxed mood.

"No. I was advised not to brooch a loan when I spoke with national project coordinator 'cause I'll be frustrated and Oga has said nothing about support" Pius rubbed his temple. He was in physical pain over this project. He'd been on paracetamol for so many days now, he was afraid he would get addicted.

"Have you tried Mama?" Seth asked casually.

"Mama? What's Mama got to do with projects?" Pius wondered.

"She's got weight brother. Heavy. I've told myself when I'm ready to cross that bridge; I'll be riding on her back"

"Mama?" Pius chuckled, unable to picture what the senior pastor's wife would have to do with buildings.

"I could fix an appointment for you. She loves challenges and vision so when you're going to see her, make sure you sharpen your talking skills" Seth teased.

"If it's about talking especially on this project, it's not a problem" Pius said.

"And make sure you have an amount in mind" Seth added.

"Like how much can she push?" Pius asked eagerly.

"How much do you need?"

"In excess of four million?" Pius said, askance.

"Ask for four. If she loves you, you'll get half in a week"

"You're kidding" Pius jumped.

"Let's fix a date with her first. I can arrange that" Seth jolted to his feet. "I'll give you a call later in the evening. I should have fixed a date by then. She likes me and I think she likes you too"

The projects committee of the mission released two million naira to Pius for his building project three weeks later. It was all he needed to take the project out of the critical stage and a little farther down. Mama's weight had spoken beyond his imagination.

The missions committee released the list of projects for the month and the transfers they recommended for it; pasted on the notice board. Jacob stood before it, his mouth drooping. Koma hills again? He couldn't believe his eyes. He'd almost gone blind the last time he visited on a mission trip when his allergies had returned with a vengeance. Even the principal of the missions' academy had recommended he be sent to an environment with less harsh climates. Another six months of being a nuisance or would to God he got a miracle. Without the miracle, he dreaded the very thought. He was supposed to be useful, to propagate the gospel, not to hibernate in a hut and leave his colleagues giving excuses on his behalf. The idea for the rotation was to help them locate their call and the area of their deepest passion. Why Koma again?

Peter trudged up to the notice board sluggishly and traced the list with his finger, a half-smile lingering lazily on his face.

"Where were you sent?" Jacob asked Peter absently. Peter had been sent on a foreign mission for the last posting to Singapore. Jacob was sure his colleague would be back home. That was why Jacob felt faint when Peter drawled,

"They want to launch Malaysia, I'll be going there"

Jacob had been rotated around the country for close to three years, against church policy of course but man-made laws could develop complications, he'd been told.

"Malaysia?"

"Yeah. You? Are you going out this time?"

"I'm back to Koma. I don't know how it happened" Jacob was close to tears. 'Suffer hardness' the dictum of the missions' academy rang in his ears. Be grateful for being counted worthy to 'go into all the world' a saucy voice rang in his head.

"You'll be fine" Peter patted his back and strolled into the administrative office of the academy to pick his letter and documents. Jacob trudged after him. When he had gone, Jacob smiled at the secretary, a young woman with a calm, pleasant face named Christy.

"Can I have my letter, please?" Jacob asked politely.

"Sure" she smiled. "Here, let me see, are you going out?"

"No" Jacob knew she meant outside the country. "Koma" he mumbled.

"Again?" Christy's head shot up to gaze at the young, enthusiastic missionary. "It must be a mistake. You just came back from Koma. Are you a perm?" she asked. Perm, shortened from permanent was the term used for missionaries who volunteered to work and live in a particular place. They were usually kept in the place and only moved when the missionary requests.

"You know I'm not" he tried to smile. God, you'll give me a miracle on this one, he thought wearily. Peter from South Africa had been sent to Singapore and now Malaysia. How? Why?

"It is well" Christy's eyes softened as she pulled out the letter from a stack.

"Thank you" Jacob said. He turned to leave but remembered he wanted to ask a question. When he turned again Christy was staring at him with pity. She understood.

"Please, Sis. Christy" he started, getting her full attention at once, "what are the criteria for posting and who makes the final decision?"

"There are no special criteria for posting. It's usually just the rotation. You go round all the mission fields and come back to either choose your perm field or you leave the academy and join another vision of the mission" she explained. "And it's the principal of the academy that has the final say, even though Papa can advise" Christy said gently.

"So Papa and Principal know about all the posting?" he asked wondering how it was possible. Principal had assured him they would send him to somewhere more 'agreeable' was the word. At least he would rest and learn and be useful.

"No. Papa does not get to see the list till its out but Mama does"

"Mama?"

"Yeah. She's been interested in the list the last three or four postings. I know she has influenced one or two" Christy said.

"Hm. Thanks" Jacob said and walked away, determined to make it.

Mama, please shift the weight a little. Let someone breathe. Still talking about positions of influence, it is unrealistic to assume or suggest that there won't be preferential treatments. Even Jesus had the 70, the 12, the 3 and the 1! As human beings, there must be some people who are close to our breasts, who lie close to us and minister to our personal needs. It will be impossible and totally absurd to equate these ones on the same scale with: either people we have never met before, or people we hold no lenience with. It's only fair to judge ourselves in this way. However, our weight should not press on people who we have not been privileged to have close associations with and this is where the test of our integrity lay. As a mother to the flock, everyone should feel our warmth; just that not everyone can; anyway, it shouldn't be for lack of warmth.

The truth is that not everyone can be close to us, and we can't have personal or privileged relationship with everyone but that kindliness that we have the capacity to demonstrate, exhibit, ooze and be an example of, should be made available to all to see. Tampering with established regulations is throwing our weight with wrong motives and partiality. We send the wrong message and build a group of distraught and offended people. Use your influence, no one can stop you. No one should ask you not to. But, I beg you; don't use it to disillusion your sheep.

The End.

If you enjoyed this book, please leave, and review and follow me on Facebook, Pinterest, LinkedIn and Instagram (Sinmisola Ogunyinka). Thank you.

ARE YOU SAVED?

All that is written in this book may not be of much use to you if you haven't yet given your life to Christ. We cannot take difficult decisions unless we have the Righteous and Wise One that is greater than the devil to help and choose for us. The Bible says that greater is He that is in us, than He that is in the world I John 4:4. And we wrestle not against flesh and blood but against principalities, against powers, against the rulers of the darkness of this world, against spiritual wickedness in high places Ephesians 6:12.

This is why I want to encourage you to take this important decision if you haven't yet given your life to Christ. I took this decision twenty years ago and I haven't regretted it even for one day. Please pray this prayer of faith if you are willing to surrender your life to God:

Lord Jesus, I honour you. I praise you and I acknowledge you that you are Lord. I know I am a sinner and I ask that you forgive me all my sins. I want you to be my Lord and personal Saviour. Wash me clean and give me grace to serve you wholly from now on. Come into my heart to reign supreme. In Jesus' name I pray. Amen.

Praise God, you are born again.

Now that you have prayed this prayer of faith, I admonish you to:

•   Get a Bible, and read it everyday (Start from the first four books of the New testament to familiarize yourself more with your new Commander-in-Chief, Jesus Christ)

•   Pray everyday.

•   Attend a Living Church

•   Introduce yourself to the Pastor and seek further teaching (you can join the foundation class and activity group in church – you are hence making yourself available to work for God)

•   Tell others about your salvation.

May God help you in Jesus' name. Amen.

THE NIGERIAN CHILD – MY VISION
Hab. 2:2 Then the LORD answered me and said: "Write the vision And make it plain on tablets, That he may run who reads it.

More than before, it's time for the well-to-do to cater for the less-privileged. Over the past few years, the Lord has laid this burden for THE NIGERIAN CHILD on my heart and I believe it's time to spread the vision. I have a desire to help and to instigate help for THE NIGERIAN CHILD. There are currently five areas of help I have been able to identify.

1.	THE MARKET-SCHOOL PROJECT: this vision is aimed at eradicating street and market hawking in the long run. The strategy is to erect schools in market places where children hawking can take a few hours out to learn and then go back to their jobs. It is a long term project and a highly capital intensive one.

2.	THE BREAD AND MILK PROJECT: bread and milk will be given in the morning time to children trekking to school just before school resumes. It can be done once a month, once a week or everyday. Or as rampantly as the provision is available. It is not very capital intensive and as little as N50 or $0.35 (US dollar) can feed a child with bread and warm milk

3.   THE UMBRELLA PROJECT: to help alleviate the suffering of children who hawk on the streets (while we work towards eradicating hawking on our streets), by providing umbrellas especially during the rainy season. The umbrellas can also be useful during the scotching hot weathers. Umbrellas of different sizes will be given depending on the size of the child. Prices of umbrellas range from N350.00 to N500.00 or $2.50 to $3.50 (US dolla

4.   THE SORT-A-CHILD PROJECT: This is aimed at helping at least a child in whatever capacity you can. It can be by paying a sick child's hospital bills, buying food and clothing for a child or paying a child's school fees. It can be as long as a life-time commitment or a one-time affair.

5.   THE STUDENT CARE PROJECT: for secondary and tertiary students who can't afford their school fees. The idea is to help through the bob-a-job initiative

THE NIGERIAN CHILD vision is not another non-governmental, money-spinning organisation. It is service to God and provision for THE NIGERIAN CHILD. It can be done privately or corporately. The important thing is to help a NIGERIAN CHILD.

I beg to challenge EVERY CHURCH IN NIGERIA to adopt the SORT-A-CHILD PROJECT or as the Lord lay it on our hearts.

HELP!

Signed - THE NIGERIAN CHILD

JUST LIKE PLAY
SHATTERED
SCATTERED

NOVELS:
TO WHERE THE WIND BLEW (BOOK 1, EIBA FAMILY SAGA)
SCENT OF WATER
PEPPER
FRAIL FLESH
THE DAYS AFTER THAT NIGHT

ISSUES OF LIFE SERIES (CO-AUTHORED WITH AFOLARIN OGÚNYINKA):
SOMEBODY HELP! SHE LOVES MY HUSBAND
SOMEBODY HELP! HE LOVES MY WIFE
SOMEBODY HELP! I'M IN LOVE
NO IS NOT NEGATIVE
SOME GOD USE, SOME USE GOD

REVELATION SERIES:
CHOICE

www.ingramcontent.com/pod-product-compliance
Lightning Source LLC
Chambersburg PA
CBHW051612120626
46551CB00014B/1755

*   9 7 8 1 9 5 9 8 3 5 2 5 7   *